MW01029534

Terrorism and the Maritime Transportation System

By

Anthony M. Davis

WingSpan Press

Printed in the United States of America.

Published by WingSpan Press, Livermore, CA
www.wingspanpress.com

The WingSpan name, logo and colophon are trademarks
of WingSpan Publishing.

ISBN 978-1-59594-236-4

First Edition 2008

Library of Congress Control Number 2008925812

This is dedicated to the men and women serving our nation in the military, law enforcement, intelligence community, fire, security and emergency management professionals.

Your sacrifice and willingness to serve is respected and appreciated.

Acknowledgment

Nothing in this text can be written without giving credit to the one who makes it possible. There were times in my life when change came as a result of promotion, military transfer, sometimes through very unhappy circumstances or just the natural course of living each day. There were times when I was unwilling to accept the change at face value. Rather than trust the one who gives all good things, I failed to see the sun and saw only the storm. I often thought the new environment would become a detriment, rather than what it eventually became.

GOD and GOD alone put me where I needed to be. He sent His Son, who saved my soul and He helped me to cope with the sometimes very rough edges. My impatience and frustration provided no value other than a slow lesson over time that He knows what is best. The lessons learned eventually provided substance for this book.

Yet I am always with you;
you hold me by my right hand.

You guide me with your counsel,
and afterward you will take me into glory.

Psalm 73: 23-24

Recognition

So many people have been a great help to me. There is no doubt that if I attempted to name them all, I would certainly fail. To the many readers of the Homeland Security Report: Thank you for sharing tips and ideas that other law enforcement and security professionals can use. As part of an international community of professionals, you help keep the globe safe from the threats of terrorism.

I certainly need to thank Mr. Robert W. Foster, Chief of Investigations with the U.S. Coast Guard Marine Safety Office in Mobile, AL. Many years ago, a promotion, (that should have been a good thing) looked like a bad situation. Bob saw something in me, stepped out on a limb and sought my transfer to the Investigations Department. Without Bob's help, so much of what has been, would never be. Thank You.

Another man, Harry Palmer in Mobile, AL has been a consistent and faithful friend over the years. Harry is a true patriot who seeks no recognition. Given that, I will not describe the specifics other than to say that his technical help is a key to the many people receiving the Homeland Security Reports each month. Thank You.

Table of Contents

Introduction

U nderstanding the maritime threat requires an historical review of criminal and terrorist elements. A closer look at the methodologies of terrorism gives greater insight to the maritime condition as it stands today. Some threats have remained for years; others are practiced daily in far away places, distant from the comfort we call our homeland.

This book will not pretend to provide answers to all of the threats we face – only provide greater magnification for understanding. Prevention comes by recognizing the possibilities and then developing sufficient contingency plans. Circumstances currently exist allowing the possibility of terrorist actions within our borders. Far too often, we allow these opportunities by living in denial, or by yielding too much latitude to groups opposed to responsible societal control.

When discussing maritime security, it is important to look far beyond maritime shipping. As a natural response, we think of ships and coastlines. The immense bodies of water surrounding our nation become mental barriers protecting us from foreign attack. The U.S. has over 95,000 miles of coastline and 361 official maritime ports of call. Our maritime interests include nearly 3.5 million square miles of Exclusive Economic Zone (EEZ). The land borders of Canada and Mexico additionally play a vital role in the Maritime Transportation System (MTS). We will look at the significance of these borders in respect to maritime security in the pages ahead.

The maritime industry is an intermodal transportation component vital to maintaining the economic welfare of the nation. The MTS includes over 25,000 miles of navigable waterways including the Great Lakes, St. Lawrence Seaway and over 3,700 marine terminals. Through 1,400 intermodal connections, the Maritime Transportation System links with over 174,000 miles of rail connecting 48 states, Canada and Mexico.

Our transportation system encompasses over 45,000 miles of interstate highways, supported by 115,000 miles of other roadways and 2.4 million miles of pipeline. Hundreds of maritime ports and the protection of federal navigational systems including locks and dams are part of the vital arteries making up the MTS.

Given the view of the Marine Transportation System noted above, the immense quantity of targets and locations exponentially multiply the potential for criminal or terrorist exploitation. As the broadened view of the Maritime Transportation System is covered, it may appear that the maritime focus is lost. These subtle shifts are intentional as it is important to show perspectives of criminals and terrorists, and show the potential vulnerabilities we face.

I expect that there will be those that disagree with some of my perspectives. Many academicians provide valuable insight to how particular terrorist groups operate and I respect that. This book comes from my experience, as a maritime investigator, and former maritime intelligence officer. The academic perspective provides a valuable baseline. My viewpoint from being on scene augments the maritime issue for better understanding. With that, it is important to note that having been within the intelligence realm, this book contains no classified information. All sources used come from open source reporting and a variety of government sponsored reports.

This text is written in three sections. Beginning with *Criminals, Terrorists and First Responder Challenges*, we will see some of the many issues for both law enforcement and the intelligence community when an event occurs. Is the event the work of criminals or terrorists? Is there a potential for a secondary attack? If so, what actions are needed? How and when can evidence be collected? You will see that the definition of terrorism is a nebulous thing. The definition changes according to who explains it. The FBI for instance has two characterizations depending upon the geographic location of the incident. I provide my own perspective and definition that merges criminal and terror events. I believe terrorism can be characterized according to who the target is and the intended outcome.

Given my definition, we will take a new look at historical crimes and discuss whether these could be classified as terrorism or not. If another terrorist attack occurs within our borders, citizens will have expectations of both the law enforcement and intelligence communities. Yet, we need to understand the challenges they face with training, developing collaborative networks and the many expectations placed upon them. I conducted a four-year survey dealing with this issue. The respondents, all of them being law enforcement, intelligence, security professionals or first responders, provided the same bleak picture of the challenges they face. In order to prevent a terror attack, we need to know what terrorism is and what our capabilities or shortfalls are. This section covers many of those issues and I fully expect this area will encompass the most debate.

The second section, *The Maritime Realm* addresses the ships and the crew that sail them. We will look at the structural condition of ships over time and some indicators of ships operated by or transporting criminal or terrorist elements. No one thought that terrorists would use aircraft as a deadly attack mechanism. We should not be so ignorant about the maritime realm. This section reviews maritime casualties and the inter-relation to terrorism. Even after the 9/11 attacks, some classes of vessels operate along our waterways with little or no oversight. This is purely the fault of lobbyists and legislators unwilling to pursue safe and secure legislation.

We will see how small vessels can become highly efficient tools of terror on the water. As we address maritime piracy, the question once again returns of where the line is drawn between criminal and terrorist activity. We will then address Liquefied Natural Gas (LNG) ships. The press and some politically focused groups have characterized these vessels as floating bombs. There are dangers associated with these vessels, but it is vital to debunk the myths and share the facts so that first responders will know the proper actions to take in the event of an incident.

The final section, *Other Issues of Concern* discusses a bacterial and non-indigenous alien species invasion that our nation faces everyday from incoming ships. The result of these daily attacks costs our national economy billions of dollars each year in damage and control costs. The environmental and economic impact eventually brought President

Clinton to draft an Executive Order to address the issue. The final portion of this section will talk about national transportation infrastructure and our vulnerabilities from within our borders as well as external elements targeting us.

As the reader, you will benefit by considering the intermodal nature of cargo from the ship to the consumer and how criminal and terror incidents abroad could be effectuated here. What areas within the Maritime Transportation System remain vulnerable? How can law enforcement prevent an incident and what should first responders do after the fact? This book provides the basic tools to answer some of those questions.

Section 1

Criminals, Terrorists and First Responder Challenges

Chapter One

Criminals and Terrorists

This book focuses on the terrorist threat and the Maritime Transportation System. While not intended to be an exhaustive analysis, it would be a failure to disregard the criminal element. The goal of this chapter is to focus the mindset to recognize the potential for an event to be criminal, terror, or both.

This prerequisite thinking will be valuable later in the book as aspects of the Maritime Transportation System are explained. Having said that, this chapter seemed to be the most time consuming of all to write. The chapter often times took on a life of its own. Many times writing stopped to regain focus, describe terrorist methodologies and attempt to show the transparency of how crime and terrorism are connected.

Terrorist groups operate using both active and passive support networks, often through many of the same criminal enterprises found in organized crime. With the establishment of international economic trade agreements to support economic growth, transnational criminal organizations quickly began to exploit new opportunities for financial gain. Free trade within the European Union (EU), the North American Free Trade Agreement (NAFTA), the fall of the Soviet Union and increased commercialization in Asia effectively unlocked the gates and opened the borders to criminal and terrorist organizations.

Another borderless environment supporting crime and terrorism was the spread of the Internet in the early 1990's. Intelligence has shown this electronic structure is used against the United States and western interests as an effective communication tool by terrorist organizations. According to Dr. Sandy Gordon, National Coordinator, Intelligence with the Australian Federal Police, there is an estimated $30 Trillion circulating the globe at any one time. These funds are transferred in the form of over 700,000 wire transfers each day.

Domestic and transnational criminal organizations use the maritime nexus each day in the fulfillment of their operations. The coming chapters will show that many times those operations support terrorism. The distinction between crime and terror becomes transparent and difficult to characterize, particularly when seeking an agreement of the definition of terrorism. To Western society, terrorism is an evil that kills the innocent and destroys culture. For some, terrorism is a useful mechanism to maintain or establish a preferred social order.

Defining terrorism has been a challenge for civilized societies throughout history. It is important to distinguish, classify and control those behaviors that threaten our human order.

The nature of terrorism fluctuates through the continual changing state of values, political systems and advances in technology. Frequently in an attempt to define terrorism, inevitably someone will use the phrase, "One man's terrorist is another man's freedom fighter." I reject that analogy. Including terrorist activity with freedom fighting is to elevate the position of cowards. Those who kill the innocent, for any reason should not receive credence as if their acts are worthy. Those who fight to defend the right to live freely are freedom fighters – not terrorists.

Many attempts to define terrorism emerged throughout the last century, all without success. The importance of a universally accepted definition allows the prosecution of acts of terrorism in a court of law. To enforce the law, a clear demarcation line must be established defining acts that are punishable offenses.

As far back as 1937, the League of Nations attempted to find an internationally accepted definition. Yet, the convention was never brought into being. The following definitions illustrate a few of the many attempts to characterize terrorism.

Definitions of Terrorism

The 1937 League of Nations convention:

> "All criminal acts directed against a State and intended or calculated to create a state of terror in the minds of particular persons or a group of persons or the general public".

U.S. Code of Federal Regulations:

> "...The unlawful use of force and violence against persons or property to intimidate or coerce a government, the civilian population,

or any segment thereof, in furtherance of political or social objectives."

FBI (Domestic Terrorism):

"...The unlawful use, or threatened use, of force or violence by a group or individual based and operating entirely within the United States or Puerto Rico without foreign direction committed against persons or property to intimidate or coerce a government, the civilian population, or any segment thereof in furtherance of political or social objectives."

FBI (International Terrorism):

"...Violent acts or acts dangerous to human life that are a violation of the criminal laws of the United States or any state, or that would be a criminal violation if committed within the jurisdiction of the United States or any state.

These acts appear to be intended to intimidate or coerce a civilian population, influence the policy of a government by intimidation or coercion, or affect the conduct of a government by assassination or kidnapping.

International terrorist acts occur outside the United States, or transcend national boundaries in terms of the means by which they are accomplished, the persons they appear intended to coerce or intimidate, or the locale in which their perpetrators operate or seek asylum."

Department of State:

> "...Premeditated, politically motivated violence perpetrated against noncombatant targets by subnational groups or clandestine agents"

United Nations:

> "...Any act intended to cause death or serious bodily injury to a civilian, or to any other person not taking an active part in the hostilities in a situation of armed conflict, when the purpose of such act, by its nature or context, is to intimidate a population, or to compel a government or an international organization to do or to abstain from doing any act."

Many of the definitions given above include political agendas as part of the modus operandi. While I believe political influences can play a strong part, limiting terrorism to political ideals alone is to invite error. The following is my definition of terrorism.

Anthony M. Davis:

> "Any act which induces pain, fear or death upon innocent citizens, a particular culture, religion or representatives of authority, or to wage destruction affecting economic commerce to support an agenda."

My definition certainly leaves areas untouched. It does however; allow the inclusion of criminal events within a terror classification. I believe the line between crime and terrorism continues to become transparent.

Terrorists are criminals, but not all criminals are terrorists. Both the criminal and terrorist wreak havoc upon societies for their own purposes. Their actions often blend in confusion with the other. The criminal seeks opportunity for personal gain, whereas the terrorist searches for opportunity to exploit vulnerabilities and plan nefarious, yet newsworthy attacks. Some criminal incidents might follow a terrorist attack, but terrorist attacks generally do not follow criminal events.

After the attacks of 9/11, thieves sought opportunities to exploit the situation. These individuals were not terrorists; they were criminals attempting to gain personal benefit upon the pain and suffering of another's loss.

After a major criminal event, terrorist members may fade into the shadows, using the environment as a surveillance opportunity to judge response operations. Effective terrorist organizations use these opportunities for intelligence collection to conduct detailed surveillance operations long before an actual strike.

Prior to the 1998 embassy bombings in Kenya and Tanzania, Anas al Liby, one of the suspected bombers allegedly carried out reconnaissance and surveillance activities near the U.S. embassy in Nairobi beginning in late 1993. Known as the technical expert in computers and surveillance for Al-Qaeda, al Liby recruited Ali Mohamed, a naturalized American from Egypt and a former U.S. Army sergeant. Together they conducted surveillance training to include map and blueprint reading and photography skills. In addition to surveillance of the U.S. embassies, he assessed other potential targets including the U.S. Agency for International

Development and other allied government buildings. Attack plans were being formulated five years prior to the actual assault. This long-term strategic approach to operations is indicative of the planning and patience by terrorists as they carry out their attacks.

My characterization of terrorism applies to criminal activity in the same way it applies to acts of terror. Terrorism is not a political issue; it is a crime. The Uniform Crime Reports published by the FBI shows no differentiation between the two. Crime is crime regardless of who does it or why. As an example, ethnic cleansing is terrorism. It is also a crime against humanity. Some terror groups if given the opportunity would emulate the same level of killing against western culture in support of their agendas.

First Responders

Local law enforcement are usually the first responders on the scene of a terrorist incident. The challenge for these personnel is accurately assessing the act and associated risks. Is it the work of terrorists or simply a criminal act? If a terrorist incident, are responders prepared for secondary attacks targeting them? The scene that appears to be a simple case of vandalism could very well be an act of domestic terrorism.

Investigators must begin with securing the scene, then stepping back to view the big picture. Identifying the target and its relation to a possible agenda can be beneficial in determining the scope of an incident. If law enforcement personnel are dealing with a terror event, response operations could easily require protection against chemical, biological, radiological hazards, or a combination of many dangers, leaving responders susceptible to exposure.

Historical Views of Terrorism

The Middle East: A common perception of the ongoing conflict within the Middle East is religious intolerance, when in fact; the tension began with issues of bloodlines. This conflict dates back to Abraham and Sarah who in their elder years could not conceive a child.

When the wife could not conceive and provide an heir, the tradition of that age was that the wife would present a slave woman to her husband for childbearing. An heir born through this union was considered a child of the wife. In this instance, Hagar the slave of Sarah was given to Abraham and bore him a son named Ishmael. The relationship between Sarah and Hagar became one of animosity and conflict; Sarah eventually sent Hagar away with Ishmael. Sarah later had a son of her own with Abraham 14 years later, named Isaac.

A key issue is that the first-born son earns the right of inheritance, in this case, Ishmael. However, the first-born, Ishmael and his mother were sent into the wilderness as illegitimate, whereas, the second born son, Isaac was treated as the rightful heir. These two sons were the genesis of two peoples – Ishmael, the beginning of the Arab race, and Isaac the Jewish race. While a number of issues pervade the historical conflict, continual tension lies in seeking legitimacy through bloodlines in the midst of a matriarchal society.

Given this view, peace is not an acceptable option to the Arab people as long as there are Jews living in regions perceived as theirs. This conflict will continue with both sides living at odds. With each violent action taken against their adversary, the number of victims continues to grow. The survivors of these actions seek revenge in the name of those lost and raise the threshold of killing to another level.

According to Human Rights Watch, looking back at a two-year period from September 2000 to September 2002 there were 55 suicide bombings in the region wounding 1,845 and killing 261 people. Of those attacks, 48 were directed against the civilian population. The number of attacks increased over 54% from 2001 to 2002. Attempts by the United States to seek peace are noble. However, other nations see U.S. efforts as meddling in other's affairs. To the terrorist, this involvement solidifies both American and other western interests as potential targets of future terror attacks.

Latin America: Many of the roots of urban terrorism began in Latin America. Ernesto "Che" Guevara, an Argentinean born revolutionary participated with Fidel Castro in the overthrow of Fulgencio Batista. Guevara believed poverty within Latin America was the result of a class conflict. To counter that, authority had to be challenged through non-conventional methods – guerilla warfare. After the successful overthrow of the Cuban government, Guevara exported his Marxist ideals to Bolivia with the formation of the National Liberation Army (ELN).

The ELN has since moved to Colombia where they remain active conducting hundreds of attacks against foreign industry, particularly petrochemical companies working throughout rural areas. According to a 1998 estimate by The Colombian Department of Administrative Security, the ELN obtained $84 million from ransoms and $255 million from extortion.

Another cog in the terrorist machine was Carlos Marighella, a Brazilian born legislator and communist. He believed the fight should be taken to the urban environment inflicting maximum damage and gaining the most attention. In 1969, he wrote "The Minimanual of the Urban Guerilla." Marighella described the urban guerilla as:

> "...an implacable enemy of the regime, and systematically inflicts damage on the authorities and on the people who dominate the country and exercise power. The primary task of the urban guerrilla is to distract, to wear down, to demoralize the military regime and its repressive forces, and also to attack and destroy the wealth and property of the foreign managers."

Since the publishing of the "Minimanual" text, both international and domestic terrorists have utilized it as a training guide. With the offensive moved into the urban realm, it quickly becomes difficult to identify terror versus criminal incidents. There are many groups throughout the world using this methodology of violence, intending to uphold a campaign of terror to suit their cause.

While there are plenty of texts covering this topic, I will stop, leaving the foundation and historical views of Middle Eastern and urban terrorism. In today's world, we continue to see a rise of terror activity brought into the urban realm. This is a continuing challenge for our law enforcement personnel as will be seen ahead.

Chapter Two

Domestic Terrorism or Criminal Acts?

On August 28, 2003, a bomb exploded outside the Chiron testing facility in Emeryville, CA. Less than a month later, another detonation occurred in Pleasanton. Law enforcement quickly linked these incidents as domestic terrorism because both facilities had ties to animal testing and the use of animal products. Was the bomber operating as part of a group or a lone wolf on a self-defined mission? According to an FBI Congressional Statement by John E. Lewis, Deputy Assistant Director, Counterterrorism, these acts:

> "...demonstrates a new willingness on the part of some in the movement to abandon the traditional and publicly stated code of nonviolence in favor of more confrontational and aggressive tactics designed to threaten and intimidate legitimate companies into abandoning entire projects or contracts."

In West Covina, California, an automobile dealership was set afire. There were 120 Sport Utility Vehicles destroyed or severely damaged. Was this simple arson or an operation by supporters of an environmental activist group? Again, this was an easy link to domestic terrorism because of the target selection and significance. In La Jolla, CA. fire destroyed a condominium complex under construction leaving an estimated $50 Million in damages. Was this the work of an arsonist, an accident caused by onsite electrical wiring, or the work of domestic terrorists?

In October 1998, Matthew Shepard, a gay college student was beaten, tied to a fence in freezing temperatures and left to die along a Wyoming highway. In June 1998, James Byrd Jr., a black man was tied to the back of a truck and dragged to his death along the road by three white men with ties to the KKK and the Aryan Nation. Were these horrific incidents hate crimes or actions sanctioned by a right wing terrorist group?

Throughout the country synagogues and churches burned. Since the 9/11 attacks, Middle Eastern citizens, their homes, businesses and mosques were targeted. Was this the work of lone wolves fulfilling a self-proclaimed mission, hate crimes, domestic right-wing action or, possibly radical Islamic groups attacking their own for choosing a western style of life? While all of these incidents were criminal in nature, these cases could also be considered terrorist events. Fortunately, law enforcement has identified the nature and motives of many of these incidents, successfully prosecuting the offenders.

These examples show that investigators must look at each incident with new eyes to recognize potential terrorist incidents. Given my definition of terrorism, "Any act which induces pain, fear or death upon innocent citizens..." violent crimes against persons could qualify as an act of terrorism.

The transparent line between terrorism and crime continues.

A view of historical terrorist methodologies have made it appear easy to define criminal and terrorist incidents into two separate camps – Criminals as opportunistic, seeking personal gain; and terrorists as focused operatives supporting a political or theological agenda.

This thinking becomes a dangerous trap. The definitions are not clearly divided as black and white. Since the Fatwa decreed by Usama bin Laden on February 28, 1998, extremists are charged with exploiting *every* opportunity to attack western civilization and Jews:

> "The ruling to kill the Americans and their allies--civilians and military--is an individual duty for every Muslim who can do it in any country in which it is possible to do it, in order to liberate the al-Aqsa Mosque and the holy mosque from their grip, and in order for their armies to move out of all the lands of Islam, defeated and unable to threaten any Muslim.
>
> This is in accordance with the words of Almighty God, and fight the pagans all together as they fight you all together, and fight them until there is no more tumult or oppression, and there prevail justice and faith in God."

This "attack at will" mentality has become a tactic of suicide bombers, making detection increasingly more problematic. With an increase of criminal intelligence methodologies and information sharing among agencies, domestic terrorism becomes more difficult to carry out. Today's terrorism is characterized in shades of grey. Law enforcement might find that a random attack is the result of an opportunity taken by terrorists.

The criminal element seeks to gain tangible reward for his or her efforts and then moves on to the next opportunity. The terrorist conducts criminal activities to finance the organization then focuses upon larger acts designed to bring fear and doubt upon innocent citizens, all the while ensuring the event has news coverage. The terrorist believes they have a called purpose for their actions, sanctioned by almighty God. In their minds, that purpose is justified.

Chapter Three

Understanding Terrorist Methodologies

This book intends to show an overview of the Maritime Transportation System and the potential for terrorist exploitation. First, we had to look at the transparency of criminal events and terrorist incidents, followed by some examples where a crime might be classified as terror related. Given that, a foundation of terrorist methodologies is necessary to understand the potential challenges ahead. From this perspective, the way that both criminal and terror groups operate can translate over to the maritime realm.

Regardless of the terrain, a terrorist group must design an effective support structure if there are ambitions of longevity. While not intending to make light of terrorism, blowing up buildings and killing people is not an economically sound business.

Recruitment, training, discipline, and logistical operations are major segments of the large pie, which must be included in the group's structure. Long before an actual attack, terrorists plan and conduct surveillance activities. Operational rehearsals continue until every event becomes second nature in the minds of the tactical personnel. Comparing this operational construct to our military Special Forces and Tactical Law Enforcement personnel, each facet of the operation is done by instinct.

The future of a terrorist group depends upon the maintenance of detailed financial networks to fund their costs. Both passive and active support chains are developed to augment the organization. Neither the active nor the passive support member actually engages in operational attacks.

Active supporters should not be confused with tactical operators. Active supporters are the recruiters and fundraisers and may participate in criminal enterprises to support the financial status of the organization. The active member may, as time goes on, shift roles from supporter to actor if they feel their contributions are not sufficient.

Passive supporters blend into society, working and living their daily lives quietly. These are the typical, "Sleepers"; passive supporters giving donations to organizations funding the group's cause. Passive supporters may also conduct long-term surveillance of law enforcement and other first responder personnel, passing the info up the chain.

Both passive and active supporters remain isolated from other divisions within the organization, maintaining a cell structure. As you will see in the next section, terrorist groups utilize these support networks to maintain the financial structure.

Financial Networks of Terror Organizations

As noted earlier, the longevity of terrorist organizations depends heavily upon financial resources. This becomes a challenge with increasing operational costs mostly conducted through covert means.

You won't find a bell-ringer with a bucket saying, "Support Terrorism" at your local grocery store. A terrorist organization recruits operatives, then must train, pay, house and feed them. The finances need to be accrued out of sight of law enforcement and intelligence agencies. The continual operational costs related to planning, travel and support expenses, often include safe houses and payoffs for information. An active terrorist organization requires a steady supply of expendable resource equipment for training, ammunition and explosives.

Today's terrorist seeks the acquisition of new technological tools and methods to gain advances over their targets. These new technologies include communications systems, computer networks, and high tech weapons, and for some - weapons of mass destruction. Costs become astronomical without financial networks securely in place and the life of a terrorist organization is short.

Both criminal and terror groups cannot operate openly; many of their financial support operations are conducted through criminal means. They operate businesses as "Fronts" to disguise other activities and logistical support. The channeling of funds are then transferred to host countries, often times through the Maritime Transportation System.

Terrorism support continues to be active within

the United States. When the U.S. Department of Treasury Office of Foreign Assets Control (OFAC) began generating lists of Specially Designated Nationals (SDN), terrorist supporters began to modify financial support methods. They have often utilized our own free democratic system against us to raise financial support through charitable donations.

Since the 9/11 attacks, two significant legal instruments, in cooperation with the USA PATRIOT Act were enacted in the fight against terrorist financing. The International Emergency Economic Powers Act (IEEPA) allows, under Presidential authority, the ability to investigate, regulate or prohibit foreign currency exchange, thereby denying support to a potential terrorist organization. Secondly, anti-terrorist legislation, "Providing material support" or a resource to designated foreign terrorist organizations is a criminal offense.

In 2001, Federal agents shut down the Richardson Texas-based Holy Land Foundation for Relief and Development. This organization was the largest Muslim support charity in the nation with additional offices in Illinois, New Jersey and California. In 2002, the Holy Land Foundation raised over $13 Million, which supported Hamas schools encouraging children to become suicide bombers.

In 2003, two Yemeni men, Mohammed Ali Hasan Al-Moayad and Moshen Yahya Zayed were extradited from Germany for conspiring to provide material support to Al-Qaeda and Hamas. Al-Moayad is an official with the Islah political party and an Imam, or spiritual leader at the al-Ihsan mosque in Sanaa, Yemen. According to a confidential informant, Al-Moayad boasted about personally delivering $20 million to Usama bin Laden raised through fund-raising efforts and money collected at the Al Farouq mosque in Brooklyn, New York.

This case is significant because portions of the USA PATRIOT ACT, specifically sections 218 and 504 allowed coordinated efforts between law enforcement and intelligence personnel. Section 218 of the USA PATRIOT ACT amended the Foreign Intelligence Surveillance Act (FISA) further justifying foreign surveillance by indicating that a, "*significant purpose*" of the surveillance is to obtain foreign intelligence information.

Yet, Section 504 is of particular value for law enforcement and intelligence coordination in the fight against terrorism. Of note, this section allows Federal Officers who conduct electronic surveillance or physical searches to "acquire foreign intelligence information to consult with Federal Law Enforcement Officers to coordinate efforts to investigate or protect against actual or potential attacks, sabotage, terrorism or clandestine activities by foreign powers." Critics of the USA PATRIOT ACT fail to see the unknown value of this important legislation in terms of potential lives saved against future attacks.

In early 2005, Al-Moyad and Zayed went to trial. Interestingly enough, the key witness and confidential informant, later identified as Mohamed Alanssi, was designated a, "Hostile Witness" after setting himself on fire in front of the White House as part of an FBI protest in November 2004. Alanssi's dramatics were non-productive. After a five-week trial, both Al-Moayad and Zayed received convictions for the terrorism conspiracy. Al-Moayad continues to claim his actions were legitimate fund-raising activities for the Yemeni people.

Both cases shown above illustrate a greater need to monitor fund-raising activities supporting foreign nations or entities. When not properly monitored, one man's charity can become a seed for terror.

Money Laundering

When international criminal or terrorist organizations pursue illicit activities like those noted above, the monetary gains are frequently laundered and smuggled out of the country. According to a National Drug Intelligence Center (NDIC) report, the Maritime Transportation System is one of the many common vehicles for exporting these funds:

> "Smuggling bulk cash and monetary instruments, such as money orders and checks, is a principal drug money laundering method used in the United States. Bulk shipments of drug proceeds are smuggled out of the United States concealed in private vehicles, commercial trucks, and air and maritime cargo; carried by couriers traveling on commercial airlines, trains, and buses; and sent through parcel delivery and express mail services. In August 2000, the U.S. Customs Service seized $11.4 million in a 6-week period as part of "OPERATION POWERPLAY," which focused primarily on drug-related outbound currency smuggling."

According to National Drug Threat Assessment of 2003, drug users in the U.S. spent nearly $64 billion on illicit drugs during 2000. The saying, "What comes around, goes around" is fair play in the money laundering mechanism. The same 45,000 cargo containers arriving in the United States each day will later depart bound for foreign destinations.

Each of these containers could be a potential delivery mechanism to smuggle currency to receiving organizations abroad.

A snapshot view of outbound currency was discovered during OPERATION IRAQI HERITAGE. In the spring of 2003, U.S. Immigration and Customs Enforcement (ICE) embedded 15 Special Agents with the U.S. Military. Their primary mission was to identify potential U.S. persons or entities illegally aiding the Iraqi regime with weapons or sensitive technologies.

Additionally, these agents sought to locate national treasures looted from the Iraqi National Museum. During the investigation, the U.S. Military and ICE agents found $788 Million in U.S. currency and 90 Million Euros stashed away in 203 metal boxes. A follow-on investigation discovered a handwritten letter by Saddam Hussein to the Central Bank of Iraq authorizing his son, Qusay to withdraw large sums of U.S. currency and Euros.

The following is the translated letter:

[Translated version]

Extremely confidential
In the name of God the most merciful the most compassionate

Mr. Governor of the Iraqi Central Bank

We are giving, with this written notice, permission to Mr. Qusay Saddam Hussein and Mr. Hekmat Mezian Ibrahiem to receive the following amounts of money:

1. Nine hundred and twenty million American dollars.
2. Ninety million Euros.

To protect and save them from American aggression Take the necessary action
[Signature] Saddam Hussein
President of the Republic
3/19/2003

[End translation]

The United States is a land of opportunity. Yet, opportunities are dependent upon choices. Live decent, productive lives, or exploit our free society for illegal gain. Transnational criminals and terrorists have long recognized these opportunities and abused them. Often times, internal liberal, "Watchdog groups" have fought for causes rather than common sense.

The resulting actions allow our adversaries greater reign against us. We should fight for freedom – freedom to be responsible, contributing members of society, not just the autonomy to live without legal oversight. If we are to overrun the terrorism machine, we need to take serious action starting with the removal of their funding.

In recent years, the U.S. Department of Treasury took positive down-to-business steps to fight terrorist financing through an initiative beginning in August of 2004. The Office of Terrorist Finance and Financial Crime (TFFC) is a proactive component seeking to gather intelligence regarding terrorist financing and disrupt their activities.

Another vital piece of the Treasury Department's

war on terror is the Office of Foreign Assets Control (described earlier). The OFAC enforces economic and trade sanctions against foreign countries, terrorists, narcotics traffickers, and those elements supporting the proliferation of weapons of mass destruction. Through the combination of the TFFC and OFAC, the Treasury Department has a viable answer to begin the fight against terrorist financing.

Terrorist Bombings

Reviewing terrorist methodologies, the historical weapons of choice for many terrorist organizations are bombs. Commonly known as Improvised Explosive Devices (IED), they are inexpensive to produce, easy to conceal and can be detonated through a multitude of inexpensive methods. Both U.S. and Coalition Forces have dealt with the effects of IEDs during the Iraq war. Many of these explosive attacks were detonated with cell phones.

In August of 2002, a bombing attack killed seven people, including five Americans at Jerusalem's Hebrew University. The bomb was triggered by a cell phone detonator. In that attack, the terror group Hamas claimed responsibility for the attack.

Terror groups realizing the benefits of remote operated devices are frequently putting them to use. Whereas suicide bombers use local detonators, the remote IEDs permit multiple attacks by the same operations personnel. This tactic allows better tactical timing, an opportunity to videotape the event for propaganda purposes, and most often guarantees escape.

With the increased use of wireless cell phones and

Radio Frequency (RF) devices, remote detonations will become a dilemma for law enforcement and security professionals seeking to protect maritime interests and infrastructure. Imagine this scenario:

Hundreds of sightseers are walking along the pedestrian path of a well-known bridge. As a large cargo ship passes below, the tourists all grab their video cameras to capture the unique viewpoint; some are talking on their cell phone. The vessel below has an IED emplaced right above the bridge of the vessel.

Moments later, a detonation occurs and the vessel drifts out of control toward a rocky shore. The ship runs aground, the hull breaches and oil pours into the waterway. During the event, sightseers videotape the event and then flee for safety. One or two of then could be terrorists. Who would know?

How would law enforcement have prevented this incident? In this scenario, the city's tourism industry relies upon thousands of visitors each year that will undoubtedly walk the bridge. Will they be required to leave their video cameras or cell phones behind? If so, on what basis would that be legal? Perhaps the explosion was detonated from another location altogether. Do you see where I am going with this? It is unlikely that law enforcement, intelligence or security professionals will have an ability or legal precedent to prevent an incident of this nature without relying upon a solid intelligence tip off.

Terror groups have historically benefited through the continued use of bombings. Their controllability offers them maximum benefit by increasing casualties. These attacks inherently induce fear as a result of the blast and ensuing devastation. Bombing campaigns generate a sense of unpredictability, leaving citizens on edge, never knowing when the next IED will go off or what locations are safe. An effective bombing guarantees media attention and becomes a psychological force multiplier giving the group the appearance of having control over their targets.

The 1993 bombing of the World Trade Center and the 1995 Alfred P. Murrah Federal Building in Oklahoma City were dramatic examples of the effectiveness of a terrorist bombing. Both incidents inflicted fear into the heart of citizens. With the sense of security stolen, Americas' comfort level was replaced with a reality that anyone can become a target. Both cases were terror attacks; they were also criminal events.

Chapter Four

First Responder Challenges

This chapter will look at a variety of challenges faced by State, Local and Federal Law Enforcement when responding to an incident. If we are to protect our Maritime Transportation System, then our responders need to have the resources and training needed to effectively deal with varying challenges on scene.

The First Responder, serving in law enforcement, fire protection and emergency management face a continual uphill battle as few receive adequate training in the differences between criminal events and terrorist incidents.

In preparation for this book, the Homeland Security Group conducted a four-year First Responder survey. Law enforcement, fire, emergency management, intelligence and security personnel were questioned through all jurisdictional sectors – local, state, federal and military. These professionals were allowed the opportunity to detail their current world of work, describe existing shortfalls and provide recommendations for future operations. This telling account indicates that after the events of the 9/11 attacks, little has changed in the overall scheme of first responder preparation.

Training

First Responders are clamoring for training. Many are unaware of available programs. They know there are training deficits, but many are unsure where to start. When training is recognized, often times, funding is unavailable or personnel not allowed to attend because of personnel shortages needed to fill duties within their jurisdictional areas.

Those that do receive training are often management personnel or a select few that go to "Train the Trainer" seminars. After a single 8-hour course, they become the "agency experts" expected to train others. In a small department, this may be workable, but what about those departments already overloaded with a continuous flow of casework?

The bread and butter of first responders is resolving bad choices of others. There is no shortage of work each day attending to the dumb things or malicious acts people do. The first responder does this daily with diminishing resources, personnel shortages and constant oversight by public expectation and the media. Our law enforcement personnel need the training but cannot be away from their posts to train. This vicious circle places our personnel in the same peril as they were before the 9/11 attacks; only now, they are more aware of their situation.

First Responders need basic training that identifies differences and similarities between criminal and terrorist events. Without an understanding of terrorism, evidence collection and protection from secondary attacks against response personnel could be missed. Terrorist events are criminal events.

Yet, many law enforcement personnel will react to an incident as a criminal event first. The event won't be treated as a potential terrorist act unless higher authority tells them afterward. With a focus upon Middle Eastern terror groups, law enforcement should be given ongoing training as a reminder that there is a potential domestic terrorism problem continuing to place our citizens in harms way.

Some examples of domestic terrorist acts by U.S. citizens include Theodore Kaczynski, known as the Unabomber, killing three people and injuring 23; The bombing of the Alfred P. Murrah Federal Building in Oklahoma City in April 1995 killing 168 people and injuring more than 500; and the July 1996 Centennial Olympic Park bombing, killing two and injuring over 100 others.

Law enforcement personnel lack training in recognizing a WMD event and the symptoms of a chemical or biological attack. Actual scenario exercises following basic training give responders opportunities to understand which agencies are participants and what expertise they can bring to the incident. This concept develops interagency relationships and a chance to learn and share skills.

Unfortunately, many scenarios are conducted using a "Table-top" approach with management representatives from participating agencies talking their way through an event. This does nothing for the first responder in the field. Nor does it teach them about how to set up a triage area, decontamination stations, and alternative methods for building evacuation, ensuring 100 percent personnel accountability, or cordoning off the area for evidence collection.

Tabletop exercises do have value during the initial exercise planning but the actual drill should be conducted in a real-life environment. Tabletop exercises often leave no room for the unexpected. How does a first responder fully grasp the situation if vital personal protective equipment fails and is no longer available? What if a communication network fails or systems are incompatible with other responders from outside agencies supporting an incident? How does a tabletop exercise overcome the potential "Shock value" during an actual incident? These issues do not get accurately played out during a tabletop exercise.

A Coast Guard member retold the story of response operations following the Alaska Air Flight 261 crash off the coast of California in January 2000. He explained how response operations were consistent until he saw a small child's shoe floating in the water. At that moment, the reality of life and death hit home and he had to step back and regroup.

The unexpected will not become evident in pre-planned exercises sitting around a table. With even the best technologies at our disposal, our successes always point back to the human element. This component must be factored into response planning.

My overall experience with tabletop scenarios has not been favorable. A main (yet unofficial) focus is frequently upon two questions: Will there be coffee and donuts available, and what time is lunch? Afterward, these exercises are always a "Success". Of course they are, they're scripted! Ask management the following day how the exercise went and it often follows with one agency talking bad about another, how they didn't know the rules, or reacted too late.

Instead of recognizing there are failures in the information sharing system, they will puff themselves up with ego. Realistically, this is a failure of leadership. I have often heard comments denigrating other agencies in front of junior staff members. How will this behavior persuade an individual to build inter-agency networks when management has already described the other organization as a failure?

A tabletop exercise is precisely where mistakes should occur. It is far better to get the issues worked out before a real incident. Perhaps it's best that some management folks stay in the office. In the field, they are more of a burden to the first responders actually doing the job.

Rather than have members come together for a tabletop exercise and, "Play Drill", each agency should be prepared to present and describe their missions, jurisdiction, legal authorities, capabilities and shortfalls. By shortfalls, I am not talking about sharing dirty laundry. If an agency describes what help they need to perform their missions, another organization may have the capability to assist. Ideally, agencies should seek to develop internship programs or be part of an inter-agency fusion center. Building professional relationships will pay large dividends if a real incident occurs.

I have seen turf wars erupt over jurisdiction at tabletop exercises. How effective can these folks be when there are real lives at stake? It is important to address these issues and be dealt with prior to tasking our first responders in a real situation. Participants should include all levels of personnel within the first responder echelon. I have often gained my greatest insight by talking to the junior people. Developing worst-case scenarios during these sessions helps to define shortfalls in training and develop inter-agency understanding.

Unless assigned to an inter-agency fusion center, many first responders lack a thorough understanding of the mission or duties other agencies perform. Law enforcement personnel for example might be inclined to call for Emergency Management personnel when in fact, the Public Health Service might be the appropriate responder, depending upon the threat.

Understanding the roles and missions of all the players is vital. Where one agency may be weak, another is strong. Unless all parties are willing to learn and honestly recognize those capabilities of other agencies, cohesion will not exist during an incident. During the next major incident, no one wants to hear, "We did a better job than agency XYZ". The public expects to hear, "We worked together as a unified team, saved lives and protected our personnel." That's what matters.

Real life on-scene exercises should be conducted regularly throughout the year in differing locations and environments. The terrorist seeks to utilize our vulnerabilities to their advantage. Therefore, first responders should be aware of the potential difficulties that compound an incident due to inclement weather or other factors. The experiential training of being there and working through scenarios is a valuable preparation in the mind of those posed with working the incident.

In 2005, Hurricane Katrina came through the Gulf Coast destroying homes, businesses and vital infrastructure. While the devastation spread from New Orleans to Mississippi, those Emergency Management personnel that worked together in Mississippi prior to the storm came back faster, whereas those unprepared in New Orleans continue to pay a price. Both states have critical shipping ports and oil and chemical facilities.

Suppose a terrorist group intended to amplify the damage of a storm by conducting targeted attacks. Is this scenario included into the response posture to protect our ports and infrastructure? Are personnel trained to detect such a plan? I doubt it.

Some cities hold annual training events giving personnel only a basic awareness of an incident when a more comprehensive training program is needed. If drills are conducted only once a year, it sends a message to field personnel that training is not taken seriously and this is just another check of the box for a qualification of federal funding. These exercises should incorporate a comprehensive training program building upon the knowledge base of the first responder.

One profession commonly excluded from training is the private security guard. These personnel are often the first responders on scene charged with evacuating a facility, helping victims and securing an area for an investigation. These professionals should not become victims themselves because they are not "Sworn" personnel, or expected to stand by on the sidelines. They are valuable resources often times, with better knowledge of the facility than local law enforcement.

There is a benefit for response planners to focus upon the critical transportation and infrastructure systems. Those representatives controlling vital traffic systems, automated bridges, locks, spillways and utilities should be included in response exercises. The industries that have power over these elements often have detailed surveillance and control monitoring systems beneficial to first responders during an actual event.

Inter-Agency Communications

After the 9/11 attacks, willingness among agencies to share information remains at a disappointing level. Comments from the First Responder survey shows local departments still receive little or no information from federal agencies and there seems to be no intent to fix it. Criminals and terrorist have made known their ability to network; yet communication between our own local and federal agencies continues to fail. Internal rivalries between "Sworn" and "Non-Sworn" personnel diminish the ability to respond to an incident and keep our personnel safe.

In a Utah Police Department, a man entered the building ranting hysterically with a briefcase in his hand. The man was subdued and personnel evacuated from the first two floors. The briefcase could easily have carried an explosive device. Yet, no one thought to tell the Non-Sworn intelligence support personnel on the third floor to get out.

On the other hand, one comment recorded in the First Responder survey stated, "I'm an Intelligence Analyst; I'm not a First Responder." This mindset is unsound. Intelligence personnel participated as responders during TWA-800, and the sniper incidents in Virginia and Maryland, among others. The Intelligence Analyst is usually one of the first resources exploited during an incident to identify the links and determine potential suspects.

Another analyst stated, "A major hurdle seems to be that any element not having a badge and credentials fails the test for being vetted as a member of the 'brotherhood' of Law Enforcement." If departments expect to have success during an incident, both sworn and non-sworn personnel first must learn to play well together in their own backyard.

In the same way that police have "Ride-along" programs, other agencies should concentrate upon similar cross-experiential training. Not many law enforcement, fire or public health personnel have spent time in an Emergency Management command center to learn and gain an understanding of other agency capabilities outside of their own duty area. Smaller departments are often excluded from training because of budgetary limitations or the ability to fill course quotas.

Many training opportunities are available by instructors that bring the course to the responder. This eliminates costs of travel and lodging. If agencies cooperate and pool training budgets together, they can each send their personnel to training. This will allow more first responders opportunities to build upon their knowledge base and builds inter-agency relationships in spite of some management's best efforts to be a hindrance.

When building interagency relationships up front, before being faced with an event, there is a greater chance of success during an incident. Although, that brings up another point, the concept of success for one agency could be defined differently than another agency. These issues should be worked out before being faced with a real incident. The Incident Command Center is the wrong place to be sharing business cards for the first time.

Communications Systems

During the WTC and Pentagon attacks, communications system failures left first responders detached from command and control personnel. In 2002, The Public Safety Wireless Network (PSWN) conducted a study of communication lessons learned from the Pentagon attack. The PSWN report detailed interoperability failures of 800MHz radio systems, forcing responders to seek alternative communications methods.

The response, incident control and fire suppression required the coordination of at least 50 public safety agencies. This included preparation of medical facilities, traffic control for response vehicles, maintenance of exclusion areas to prevent public and media interference and status reports of hazardous material concerns and additional resource requests. Yet, communications systems failed.

Within the first few hours, alternative commercial service providers saw a doubling of the normal call volumes. Cingular, the nation's second largest provider at the time saw a 400 percent increase in call usage. The Public Switched Telephone Network is an important element for cellular connectivity that quickly became overwhelmed. The network saw delays, interruptions and connectivity difficulties. The system was neither designed nor prepared for such a high demand.

Lessons from a previous incident became the foundation of change for responders in the

Washington, DC area. Nineteen years earlier, on January 13, 1982 the capitol city was facing a severe winter storm. With the temperatures in the low 20's and over 25-inches of snow on the ground, a Boeing 747 prepared for takeoff.

Air Florida flight 90 was one the last aircraft to depart Washington National Airport prior to closure. Anti-icing had not been turned on, affecting the lift of the aircraft. In addition to potential icing issues, the aircrew chose to veer from flight manual guidance by using reverse thrust to assist a ground tug attempting to pull the plane from the gate. The reverse thrust caused an additional buildup of snow and ice in the engine causing an incorrect compressor inlet pressure reading. False indications, icing and misinterpretation of control instruments by the crew resulted in a loss of power and lift. The plane came down directly on top of the 14th street Bridge, a major transportation artery between the Virginia suburbs and the city, crushing four vehicles before sliding into the Potomac River. All told, 78 people were killed.

Then, approximately 29 minutes later, the Washington Metro rail system had a derailment killing three people and injuring 25. The accident occurred in an area shared by two commuter routes, the Orange and Blue lines. In less than 30 minutes, Washington area responders were tasked with two serious incidents shutting down major transportation systems during inclement weather. As they began to respond, they quickly realized that each agency had their own communications systems and frequencies limited to their own jurisdictions.

The Air Florida crash and Metro rail derailment began a series of new initiatives for interoperability between public safety agencies in the region. The following year, the Washington DC Council of Governments coordinated mutual-aid agreements, seeking to address communications issues.

By the mid 1990's, additional agreements were established allowing public safety agencies to operate on another's frequency outside their jurisdiction. Additionally, the public safety community in the Washington DC area held frequent training exercises helping to familiarize personnel with communications systems interconnectivity and training of the Incident Command System (ICS) structure.

The coordinated efforts developed since the Air Florida incident allowed for many successes years later during the initial Pentagon response. Even so, many of the connectivity problems arose when additional resources were requested from outlying areas. The Virginia State Police for instance, were unable to communicate with on-scene personnel. Their communications systems were not compatible with the regional structure used by local personnel.

Additional communications equipment had to be located and pulled from warehouses in outlying areas, programmed for compatibility and issued to newly reporting responders. As numerous phone networks began experiencing connectivity issues, major commercial service providers volunteered their equipment and personnel to maintain mobile cell sites. Their successful volunteer efforts and capabilities give credence to including these commercial providers in large-scale exercises.

While there were many communications shortfalls during the Pentagon response, many issues were identified and resolved following the 1982 incidents. Preprogrammed regional communications networks, and interagency agreements, consistent training and a Unified Command structure all served as an example to others. Many cities have not experienced a "Flight 90" – nor should they have to. An historical look at successes and failures from previous incidents can save responders the pain of learning the hard way.

Effective interoperable communications systems are a vital element of our national response infrastructure; they keep our first responders informed and safe. Yet, many agencies and municipalities have chosen systems based upon budgetary constraints with little thought for the need of a unified command system. Unless there is a standardized national interagency protocol defined and agreed upon, our first responder's safety and effectiveness will be limited by funding, information sharing failures and bad choices.

Equipment

The Council on Foreign Relations reported that the "United States is dangerously unprepared to handle a catastrophic attack on American soil." The report cites shortages of communications equipment for fire personnel, lack of personal protective equipment for law enforcement needed during a WMD incident, inabilities of public health agencies to adequately detect chemical or biological agents and shortages of training among hazardous materials responders.

In 2003, the House of Representatives introduced the Public Safety Interoperability Implementation Act. This step addresses many of the communications failure issues noted during the 9/11 World Trade Center response and appropriates grant funding to support first responder needs.

Comments from the First Responder survey however, tell that the equipment and funding needed to keep them safe has yet to arrive. In response to the question asking what major challenges they face, the following comments are consistent with the hundreds of comments obtained:

"My own department had 5 previous grants to the one we have now, beginning in 1994, for computers in the cruisers. We still don't have them."

"Like any other agency budget issues are always a concern. Doing more with less is status quo. It's to the point where we are stretched to our limits. "

"We face a lack of funding to properly equip my officers and have negative thinking public officials who think it can't happen here so we don't need it."

"We have a severe shortage of funding for both equipment and manpower for homeland security issues, i.e. guarding marine terminals, Dams, bridges, etc."

If we are to have an effective response to the war against terror, our personnel must be funded, trained, equipped and protected.

On Scene

A difficult task lies in the hands of first responders to recognize a criminal vs. terror incident quickly while at the same time control the situation and save lives. How does a crime scene remain preserved when fire and rescue personnel trample upon crucial elements critical to an investigation? Fire hoses and personnel can easily wash significant trace elements away. Yet, these responders cannot just sit back and hope a fire will go out to allow evidence collection.

During the first World Trade Center bombing of 1993, law enforcement needed to make a best guess determination whether the event was the result of a disgruntled employee seeking revenge against a business, or the work of terrorists. Responders cannot choose the situations they react to, but they can select the best options if trained and equipped properly.

Another problem is an effective counter response posture. Successful terrorist factions develop intricate intelligence collection teams focusing upon first responders and their methods. Who is going to watch the backs of law enforcement, fire and rescue personnel when their attention is upon controlling the incident?

The First Responder Survey presented participants with the question, "Are First Responders protected from secondary attacks during a possible Criminal or Terrorist incident?" Of those who respond to incidents, 91 percent believe they are lacking sufficient protection from an attack during a response.

If our law enforcement personnel are to be protected, there must be an understanding of the methodologies of terror attacks and a study those tactics used in the Middle East, Colombia and other parts of the world. Secondary attacks against first responders, sometimes using response vehicles in other parts of the world are common.

On a January 1997 morning in Sandy Springs, GA, a bomb exploded at the Northside Family Planning Clinic shortly after 9:00 am. About 90-minutes later, a secondary bomb exploded in the parking lot. The two bombs were constructed differently. Unlike the first bomb, the second explosive in the parking lot contained shrapnel. The bomber knew first responders would arrive at the scene. This bomb was for them.

Al-Qaeda has repeatedly used secondary attacks in their desire to kill first responders. The 1998 car bombings at the both of the American Embassies in Nairobi, Kenya, and Dar es Salaam included secondary attacks. During the investigation of the 1993 World Trade Center bombing, Investigators searched a storage area rented by Mohammad Salameh, one of the suspected bombers. The search discovered 250 pounds of sulfuric acid, and numerous containers, some, containing nitric acid and sodium cyanide.

No conclusive evidence exists showing usage of chemical weapons during the 1993 incident. Yet, Ramzi Yousef, a key planner of the attack told a Secret Service Agent that he would have included cyanide in the bomb if he had enough funding. This could have killed hundreds, including first responders arriving at the scene.

A look at explosive laden ambulances used in the Gaza Strip, and frequent attacks on police in Afghanistan, Colombia and Iraq show that first responders can be primary targets for attack. The Chechen bombing of a hospital and the planned attack against a medical facility in Germany also indicate that health professionals are vulnerable.

Local law enforcement and fire departments remain unprotected. Commercially available surveillance equipment sold on the Internet risks an operational security posture leaving first responders in harm's way. Interviews and surveys conducted in preparation for this text reveal that many senior leadership personnel throughout local, state and federal sectors act as though a terrorist attack would never occur in their area. The fact is it has happened to us. The WTC attacks, the Pentagon, Murrah building, U.S. embassies and interests overseas happened to us, not someone else.

Additional research of first responder challenges looked at the perceptions of law enforcement, intelligence personnel, security, fire, emergency management and military sectors. The respondents addressed hindrances to response operations, including media interaction, public and self-expectations. Results from the first responder survey indicated that 91 percent felt the media could be a hindrance preventing personnel from adequately controlling an incident. Aside from media interference, the response personnel on scene are challenged when attempting to maintain the integrity of an investigation.

A TWA-800 Lesson

I learned a valuable media lesson years ago. In July of 1996, I was the Combat Watch Officer onboard the *Coast Guard Cutter Harriet Lane*. We were patrolling the New York coast as part of a fisheries enforcement mission. The watch was quiet and uneventful and we had two smaller Cutters working with us pre-positioned in different operating areas.

At approximately 2114, I received a radio call informing us a 747 aircraft had crashed and we proceeded toward the scene. I immediately contacted the *Coast Guard Cutter Adak* by radio and told them to proceed to the area. They were the closest Cutter near the scene to respond. The *Adak* indicated that they were already en route. I'm not sure if they were called previously by the District One controller in Boston, or if they heard my exchange on the radio. We monitored the same communications frequency. Moments later, the *Adak* called back describing fire, wreckage and bodies in the water. We knew that this incident, known as TWA-800 was going to be a big one.

As I've seen many times before, Coast Guard personnel jumped to the task without question. Over the years, I've begun to believe that Coast Guard men and women have an extra portion of adrenaline allowing them to work for hours and stay focused. We began developing search plans, air and surface exclusion areas, and we established and coordinated the communications and reporting protocols for additional assets responding to the scene. The following day a weather front came through the area adding to the difficulties of rescue and recovery efforts.

The watch personnel worked around the clock coordinating assets, tracking wind and currents and relocating search areas along with the dispersed path of the debris fields caused by the weather. In situations like this, responders first operate on the adrenalin and instinct. Then, they are moved by will. Many of our watch personnel were literally given orders to get some rest. This was going to be a protracted operation and we needed to ensure our efforts were well thought out and productive.

Then, new orders: We were to become a media platform and host some 50+ print and television news personnel. We were the operators that faced the issues and ever-changing missions each day. Now we were to become a public relations platform just because some desk-sailor thought it was a good idea.

As some media representatives were granted access to the control center, sensitive equipment was turned off or covered. All secure communications would cease during their stay, limiting our ability to coordinate efforts. In a sense, we were caught in the middle. We all understood the severity of the situation. Everywhere we looked, there was debris around us. Coast Guard personnel deal with exigent circumstances every day and we so much wanted to hear of just one survivor in that mess.

We also saw the national significance, as the possibility of terrorism still existed. This was an important story and America and the world wanted to know. During one interview with a popular news show, the interviewer from a major television news show endeavored to turn my words into something untrue regarding the "Black Boxes".

The reporter asked me when divers would be in the water. I explained that the Navy was proceeding to the area with side-scan sonar and they were two days away. Divers would most likely not enter the water looking for recording devices until something was found.

Even though the Navy was two days out, the reporter continued to ask, "So, does that mean the divers will be in the water today?" "No" I said, "the Navy is not on scene yet, we are looking at a depth of about 132-feet and the weather is reducing visibility." The reporter followed with, "So they will be in the water tomorrow?" As frustration began to build within me, I finally told her that, "the American people do not want their tax money spent frivolously so divers can just swim around and hope they'll find something. The divers will do their jobs once something is found."

I was unwilling to be manipulated for the benefit of this story and the interviewer finally gave up. I never saw or heard about the interview. I'm sure my comments made it to the cutting room floor during editing. Yet, we still had a job to do and the media story seemed to be the priority. I have to admit, I did receive satisfaction when some of the reporters left seasick because of the bad weather. We then went about what we do – our jobs.

The second area of hindrance viewed during the First Responder survey was public expectation. Of those participating in the First Responder survey, 87 percent feel public expectation was an encumbrance. Popular television shows like CSI, Cold Case Files and others solve crime within neatly packaged 60-minute periods. These shows make for great entertainment, but they are not always accurate. I'm sure that many within the intelligence community wish they had the super computers that the TV cops use to identify suspects in seconds.

The public fails to realize the long hard efforts required by law enforcement to develop case evidence into something workable. They fail to see the many shortfalls in training, funding or equipment. Just because Hollywood does it within an hour doesn't make it accurate. The public expects law enforcement to resolve a situation quickly...as long as it doesn't come too close to the public's expectation of privacy.

A unique dilemma exists when groups within our own society expect the government to protect them on one hand and cry of freedom abuses on the other. Law enforcement attempts to utilize new technologies for their safety. Yet, are chastised if those same technologies get too close to home. Many in today's society have confused First Amendment rights with personal responsibility.

During the 2003 Anti-War protests in San Francisco, protestors defecated in public places, calling it their right of free speech. Properties were damaged, transportation routes blocked and commerce stopped, keeping workers from their jobs. In the midst of the many anarchists sponsored protests, the public expected first responders to bring resolution. Public expectation has become so much of an issue for first responders, it is a key element in many Criminal justice programs today.

Many of today's younger generation see protection against crime and terrorism as "Somebody else's job". After retiring from the military, I accepted a position as Federal investigator for the Coast Guard (and later, Department of Homeland Security). One day while riding the commuter train, a young man in his early twenties noticed that I was wearing a Law Enforcement style coat. He immediately began his well-rehearsed soapbox speech so others on the train could hear him. He went on about how the only thing that law enforcement and the Department of Homeland Security was good for was to make people wait in longer lines at the airport.

After a few minutes of his foolish ranting, I asked him what he was doing to keep this nation safe. He said, "Nothing. That's YOUR job". I then asked him how he is serving the nation that gives him the right to speak freely. He once again said, "Nothing that's YOUR job". He looked around the train with a big smile on his face, proud of his answer. He expected to see agreement from the other passengers. He quickly realized that everyone saw him as the selfish punk he is; he shut up and got off at the next stop.

The fact is our responders are always in the middle. Law enforcement is expected to resolve (or prevent) situations as long as they stay within predetermined guidelines set by liberal groups that breed irresponsibility. Today's protestors, anarchist groups and other idiots work hard to confuse illegal action with free speech, leaving the first responder in harm's way.

The final area of the First Responder Survey deals with self-expectation. The men and women who have chosen service professions are the rescuers, often far too busy to worry about themselves. This heroic concept is admirable, even though they sometimes place themselves in jeopardy. Of the respondents of the survey, 94 percent admit their own self-expectations during an event can in fact, be a hindrance. The reality is that many law enforcement, fire and other response personnel continue to place themselves aside in order to help those in need.

The cycle of self-expectation for the First Responder has a cumulative effect over time. If left unchecked, results will manifest health issues and destroy the personal lives of our personnel. First responders have allowed themselves to buy into the myth that doing more with less is the norm.

Coupled with the previous discussion of public expectation and the misguided self-requirement to always be a superhero, they are driven by purpose and the realization that without their efforts, our society can easily run amuck. Over time, this places them in jeopardy. Even the best well-oiled machine needs good oil. Law enforcement personnel need three important components of that oil: Rest, Respect and Resources.

Section 2

The Maritime Realm

Chapter Five

The Ships and Marine Safety Inspections

At any moment in time, thousands of merchant ships are crossing the seas, following coastlines, transiting under bridges, over tunnels, along rivers, through bays and harbors, or resting in anchorages or at piers loading or unloading cargo. The heartbeat of maritime shipping never sleeps.

Before exploring external sources that may target vessels, this chapter will first look at operations, management and inspection issues of the ships themselves. In the next chapter, we will look at the crews that sail them. The complexity of cargo vessels could easily fill a library. Given that, I believe this section will be more effective by narrowing the focus with my own first-hand inspection accounts.

Cargo ships are often built in one country with foreign laborers, owned by a holding corporation within another country, administrated under the classification society of a third country, fly the flag of a fourth country, operated by mariners from many different nations and be subject to regulatory control in each foreign port.

The operations and management of a vessel becomes a complex issue. The intricacies are readily apparent when it comes to determining the responsibilities of maintaining a security posture consistent with regulation. When there are discrepancies, it sometimes becomes a finger-pointing game between the owner and the operating company.

Because of the varying environmental conditions cargo ships encounter, maritime safety inspections are vital to ensure safe navigation at sea. Typically, the main emphasis is upon the hull, lifesaving, structural fire protection, watertight integrity, engineering equipment and the electrical condition of the vessel.

As a ship moves through the seas, the vessel endures varying stress loads impacting the overall structural condition. Fuel, water and ballast tanks face a liquid stress load from differing hydrostatic pressures exerted against the tank walls. The ship's hull and structural members are constantly twisting and flexing in a downward and upward motion, referred to as, "Hogging" and "Sagging."

With each movement and vibration, the stress travels throughout the vessel testing the welds and straining the structural integrity. Storm conditions exacerbate the potential for structural failure even further. As the vessel pitches and rolls in the seas, the weight of the superstructure, deck mounted cargo, cranes and equipment, containers or deckhouses constantly shifts, placing additional tension upon the ship.

As large waves strike the vessel, they exert both heavy weight and force against the ship. According to a detailed study of the physical characteristics of seawater at the University of British Columbia, surface waves can have a weight of 1,029 kilograms per cubic meter (2,268 lbs.) With each blow, they risk structural failure of the outer hull.

Likewise, high winds compress against the hull of the ship as vertical surfaces in effect become a large sail area, impacting maneuverability forcing the vessel off course. The wind pressing along the side of a vessel could easily have a force of 30 pounds per square foot. Given that, a 900-foot cargo ship in a storm would constantly face a structural force of many thousands of tons.

The previous narrative of stresses upon the ship emphasizes the need for regular recurring inspections. Without a detailed look at the condition of the ship, the necessity for repairs remains unknown. Over time, as the vessel continues to operate, it will endure fatigue and deteriorate.

In 1997, the *Leros Strength*, a 22,000-ton bulk carrier with a crew of 20 sailors was lost. The Captain called for help stating they were taking on water from a hole in the bow. Three minutes later, the ship flooded and sank in 20-foot seas. The Investigative report from the Norwegian Maritime Directorate described how the vessel had a series of incomplete surveys and most notably, deficiencies with a forward hatch, in effect opening a door for flooding.

Years ago while attending the U.S. Coast Guard Marine Inspector Course, a video from a rescue helicopter showed a vessel in trouble. The 900-foot bulk carrier was taking on water.

The Captain, attempting to save the vessel,

called back declining a rescue. According to the Captain, he said he was returning to port. Within moments, a large wave hit the vessel head-on and the ship lumbered in the sea and descended like submarine. The ship and the entire crew were lost within seconds, never to be seen again.

As a reader you may be asking, "What does this have to do with terrorism?" Bear with me; you'll see where I'm going. Terrorist groups that plan and successfully carry out attacks do so by exploiting vulnerabilities.

The construction of a new vessel is in accordance with the regulations for maritime construction. As an example, the Oil Pollution Act of 1990 originated from the Valdez oil spill. According to the requirements, new vessels must have double hulls and bottoms. However, older vessels still in operation can hold off until 2015. Groundings by single-hull ships can cause serious environmental and economic damage if carrying noxious chemicals or petroleum-based products. These older ships with greater vulnerabilities are precisely the types a terrorist group would seek.

As we've seen earlier, ships fatigue over time. Given that, newer vessels carry the more expensive cargoes and crude oils, whereas an older vessel will transport a shipment yielding lower profits. The decreased earnings force shippers operating on a tighter profit margin to avoid detailed inspections and costly repairs.

Likewise, the same shippers making fewer profits pay their crews lower wages, in effect recruiting the lesser experienced or those sailors unable to gain employment with more reputable companies. We'll look at the veracity of the crew in the next chapter. For now, let's continue and look at some challenges faced by marine inspectors.

There is a multitude of inspection issues onboard ships. In order to adequately describe the access and ability to perform a thorough inspection, the next two examples come from personal experience.

Prior to becoming a Coast Guard Marine Investigator, I worked as an Inspector for the first year. I conducted inspections of new vessels during construction, older ships in dry-dock, internal tanks of tank ships and other vessels and barges after collisions, groundings or other casualties. This perspective from an inspection and regulatory viewpoint provided a good baseline of understanding later as an investigator.

The Inspections

A cargo ship literally has hundreds of hatches, access plates, compartments, tanks or voids (unused spaces). For the marine safety inspector conducting structural surveys of the ship, it is a daunting task not to miss anything as the following examples show.

The internal inspection of an oil tanker began with an 80-foot climb down a vertical ladder. As I descended further into the tank, the visibility continued to darken. Holding tight with each downward step I ensured one arm was hooked into the rung just in case I lost my step. The ladder was slippery and still had traces of oil. It was like entering a dark, surreal world. The only sound was air blowers on the upper deck feeding fresh air into the space. Without them, the atmosphere would quickly become oxygen deficient. Often times, the only light was the intrinsically safe, explosion-proof flashlight in my hand.

On that day, there were four of us within the dark steel chasm of the ship. We were to inspect the welds from the inside of the tank. The four of us, three Coast Guard Inspectors and an American Bureau of Shipping (ABS) surveyor met in the center of the tank and decided upon an inspection plan. We each were to take a corner and work toward the other inspector on the same bulkhead.

At our feet were large "Lightering Holes." These twelve-foot long by four-foot wide openings in the deck led to another 80-foot drop into the subdivided tank below us. One misstep would be a sure killer. In effect, these holes were in place to act as a giant baffle, allowing an easy flowing of oil when the ship moved. If large volumes of liquid slosh back and forth within the tank while sailing, the ship would become unstable, safe navigation nearly impossible and the constant impact would eventually tear the ship apart.

We worked for hours in the dark abyss precariously climbing steel beams along the bulkheads and inspecting every weld we could reach. At one point, I was standing near the ABS surveyor when he almost stepped into one of the holes. He tried to catch himself and I grabbed his collar; it scared the heck out of the both of us. Tempt fate too much and fate will win. That was enough for one day; we climbed out. Chances are there were hundreds of welds we missed during that inspection. In that dark environment, you do the best you can.

During another inspection of a freight ship, we conducted an internal survey of the lowest portion of the ship. The dark, cramped area referred to as the "Double-bottom" redefined the meaning of dark. In order to access this area we descended ladder after ladder until we could go no further. Bolted into the deck was a small two-foot round access plate. This would be my entrance; about 100-feet away was another entrance for the other inspector. We would enter, conduct our structural inspection, meet in the middle and then back out.

The area was sealed shut for at least five years and no air circulated in this dark place. Blower fans were put in place to circulate fresh air. Without them, an inspector would suffocate within minutes.

After a 15-20 minute wait, we checked our flashlights (and backups), clipped on portable oxygen detectors and climbed into the hole. It was like climbing into an abandoned crypt – cold, dark and dirty. The air was thick and had an odd rust-metallic taste. Standing by at the deck above was another inspector. His job was to ensure no one re-installed an access plate, trapping us in. In a shipyard environment, so much is happening at any one time, this is a very real possibility.

Another option is the potential for malice. A marine inspector has a lot of power. If they find serious discrepancies, they can force the ship to stay in port until the completion of repairs. Shipboard maintenance is costly and each day at the pier is a day the ship fails to earn money.

One shipyard inspector told me of an experience when was trapped inside a tank during an internal inspection. He recently had disagreements with shipyard workers when he required them to redo their work. If it were not for other workers that heard him banging on the inside of the heavy steel plate, he most surely would have died. These things go through your mind as you enter the darkness of the double-bottom.

As I climbed down into the tight 2-1/2 foot high crawlspace the flashlight that normally shined 30-feet seemed to barely light a path just five-feet ahead of me. The area literally absorbed the light – not a place for anyone who is claustrophobic. Every few feet there was a large cross-member ahead of me to crawl over. The huge I-shaped beam was one of the many ribs of the ship's skeleton. With each climb, I moved further away from the access hole and fresh air behind me.

Focusing on the welds and structural condition, I kept moving forward. I was far enough into the space that there was now no light behind me and no sign of the other inspector's light ahead. The airflow seemed nearly non-existent. I was covered in rust, dirt and sweat. I stopped to get my bearing in the dark and hoped the break would calm the rising anxiety.

An inspection in this area is vital to ensure the vessel is structurally sound, yet, it was like being alive in a buried coffin – no apparent path out and no one to hear you. I called ahead to the other inspector but the sound seemed to go nowhere. My own voice echoed against the dark steel within the tight space. Another rest, more weld inspections and over another beam.

I must have hit a section of dead air because the oxygen sensor clipped to my coveralls began to chirp intermittently. It's normal to have false readings so I waited and the sensor ceased. I climbed over another beam and then the sensor rang out with a constant alarm. "That's it, I'm out of here!" This was one of those, "What the heck am I doing here moments."

Scrambling over beams, banging my head, knees and elbows, I finally saw the exit ahead and made my way out. As I sat on the deck with my legs hanging in the hole, I was covered in dirt, sweat, out of breath, feeling exhausted and a bit ashamed of myself for not "sticking it out." Then, looking toward the other opening in the deck, I noticed the other senior inspector looking just as hot, dirty and sweaty as I was. He had conducted many of these confined space inspections over the years whereas I was just a newbie at this game. Like me, his oxygen alarm sounded and he had to back out.

The point of this narrative is to describe the environment where inspectors have to work. Often times, the inspection process becomes an exercise of just getting through it. As noted with the internal tank inspection earlier, it is very easy to miss potential structural issues.

Coast Guard Marine Inspectors face these life-threatening challenges every day and are constantly exposed to environmental hazards and chemical substances. An Archives of Environmental Health report addresses mortality among Coast Guard Inspectors:

> "Comparison of the mortality experience of marine inspectors with other Coast Guard officers uncovered excess mortality among inspectors from cancers of the colon, liver, skin, and lymphatic and hematopoietic systems (particularly leukemia), which could

be related to organic solvents and other chemicals to which they are exposed while inspecting ships and barges."

A Review

This chapter gave just a few examples of the complexity of ensuring vessels are safely maintained and operated. With even the best efforts, inspectors are unable to fully guarantee a vessel is free of structural damage. The very nature of operating a ship in extreme weather conditions increases fatigue upon structural elements.

It's also important to remember that moving cargo within the maritime nexus is all about business. If vessels are not moving cargo, they are not making money. Inspectors working to do the best job they can are always under pressure by the ship's management and sometimes their own chain of command. If a shipper faces too many enforcement actions, delays, or mandated repairs, the profit margin declines. The shipper may then opt to conduct business in other ports, in effect decreasing the employment and economic base at stricter ports. When the economy is affected, politics always gets in the way. In the end, inspectors will hear word of vessels shipping to other ports. Stringent inspections and enforcement will ease.

The attempt to find a balance between maintaining financial opportunity for shippers and maritime safety opens the door for criminals and terrorists. As we've seen earlier in the chapter, many areas on ships are difficult to reach and inspect. Some are not inspected at all except during specified times.

While sensor technologies exist for the identification of radiological materials, drugs and some explosives, it is difficult to detect the presence of specific biological agents or chemical substances unless enforcement personnel know exactly what they are looking for and where to look. Given that, effective vessel inspections, repairs and marine safety enforcement are vital to ensure the safe operation of the maritime nexus for our nation and the free world.

Unfortunately, we still lack sufficient numbers of qualified inspectors and investigators. Both marine inspectors and investigators require a great deal of training and fieldwork to become qualified. Even if we had sufficient numbers of qualified personnel, current technologies still hamper our ability to detect some WMD threats at sea.

Chapter Six

<u>The Sailors</u>

When a mariner seeks employment onboard a vessel, they must show their level of proficiency. The proof is the documentation they present. The merchant marine world is not unlike a military structure when it comes to mariners. Some carry a Merchant Mariner's Document (MMD) and others, a Merchant Mariner's License. The difference between these documents is, in effect, the difference between the enlisted and the officer ranks.

The holder of an MMD may be a deckhand, steward, engineman, apprentice or any such position. Those occupations considered officers are the Master, Mate, Engineer, etc. They carry licenses. In order to be eligible for employment or elevation to higher positions, mariners must have appropriate sea time on the specific types of vessels where they hope to work, in addition to successfully completing a variety of training programs. For a professional mariner, their experience and training is one building block after another that takes years to accrue.

Given that, an impatient sailor would rather cheat the system. The Seafarer's International Research Centre conducted a study of fraudulent and forged documentation. They found counterfeit documentation and forged information attesting to qualifications or sea time not earned. In some cases, the mariner bought a passing grade.

When mariners arrive onboard a vessel with illegal documentation, they compromise the safety of the vessel and the crew. His or her co-workers have no idea what the skill level of the new person may be. Onboard ships, there are a multitude of ways to kill yourself or someone else if you don't know what you're doing. Mariners claiming false experience are a walking safety hazard to themselves and those around them.

In January 2006, a water taxi near Staten Island called the "Little Lady" sustained a marine casualty in the Hudson River in winter. The Coast Guard Investigation discovered that the pilot was operating and transporting passengers with a fraudulent Coast Guard Master's license.

In this case, the mariner illegally claimed a qualification to pilot a passenger vessel. He was moving passengers across the icy waters of the Hudson River. While the potential for disaster was great, the mariner only considered illegal income. The Coast Guard later referred the case for criminal enforcement and the mariner served five months in jail.

The obtaining of fraudulent maritime certificates is easy, and there is big money for those that proffer them. In December 2001, investigators arrested two Coast Guard civilian employees from the San Juan, Puerto Rico office. They charged fraudulent fees, embezzled $367,165 and provided hundreds of illegally issued USCG licenses and documents. They stole 650 blank Merchant Mariner's Licenses and obtained an MMD production machine.

The Coast Guard Investigative Service began a review of every license and MMD issued from the San Juan office. Of the 650 licenses and 957 MMDs reviewed, the Coast Guard seized 318 licenses and 256 MMDs. The two employees put 574 illegal crewmen onboard vessels.

It would be reassuring to know mariners serving onboard passenger, freight and tank ships undergo a thorough criminal background check. Unfortunately, that's not always the case. As a rule, because of the large volume of mariners applying for merchant documents, approximately 10 percent are reviewed for criminal histories. That means that 90 percent of the mariners that are seeking to avoid the law, the IRS, spouses or their attorneys could find seagoing positions as their refuge. According to the current Code of Federal Regulations, the Coast Guard, "*May* conduct a criminal record review and conduct a safety and security check of an applicant for a merchant mariner's document."

On a quiet July Sunday morning in 1966, one merchant mariner made national attention. He brutally stabbed and killed eight nurses in a peaceful South Chicago suburb. The sole survivor of the attack, a young nurse from the Philippines hid under a bed during the killings. Her description helped police when checking the nearby National Maritime Union. Stapled to a recent application for a merchant seaman job was a picture of the suspect, Richard Speck. Police were already looking to question him for the disappearance of three young girls. Speck had worked on a vessel in the town just 12 days earlier.

Police in Michigan also wanted to interview him for the Benton Harbor murders of four females aged 7, 19, 37, and 60. Onboard a ship docked in the area was Richard Speck. Police wanted to question him in connection to the Monmouth, Illinois beating death of a barmaid in April and the attack and rape of a 65 year old widow five days later. Like the other incidents, Speck was in the area and later departed on an iron ore ship. For Speck, employment at sea offered travel and a hunting ground for victims.

Twenty-five years later, patrons enjoying their lunch at a small diner in Killeen, Texas became victim to another mariner with problems. George Hennard drove his truck through the window of the Luby's diner, jumped out and began the shooting of 40 people, killing 23. Years earlier, the Coast Guard revoked his merchant mariner's document for marijuana use.

For two other famous killers, speculation continues regarding James Earl Ray and Jack the Ripper. Ray, who killed Dr. Martin Luther King, maintained he was a merchant seaman; however, union records could never validate his claims. Trevor Marriot in his book *Jack the Ripper: The 21st Century Investigation* asserts the infamous London killer was a merchant seaman. Marriott, a retired British homicide detective used modern day investigative tools to review the century-old case, naming several ships in the London area at the time of the murders. While the "Ripper" association is speculative, it does open the door to serious consideration that criminal elements could use the maritime nexus for their hunting ground, exploits, and escape.

In December 2002, I was a civilian Marine Investigator with the Coast Guard. That month the Coast Guard in cooperation with the FBI and the National Joint Terrorism Task Force (NJTTF) began, "Operation DRYDOCK," a screening of over 220,000 mariners operating on U.S. vessels. During the operation, criminal background checks were conducted on every mariner holding an MMD. If it was determined that a mariner had a criminal conviction and did not disclose it, we called them in.

This is not to say that all mariners must be "conviction free." The law only states that they must have disclosed the conviction when applying for their documents. If a mariner tells the Coast Guard reviewer they have a prior conviction, the examiner compares the crime against a table of assessment periods. As an example, a mariner with a prior aggravated assault conviction is required to wait between 5 and 10 years to reapply for an MMD. Requests outside those assessment periods prompt an additional review to ensure rehabilitation and that the mariner is no longer a threat.

Operation DRYDOCK quickly made Coast Guard investigators very busy. In addition to investigating vessel and personnel casualties, we were constantly working enforcement cases for the never-ending flow of mariners failing drug tests. The law requires mariners to undergo random, post-casualty, and pre-employment drug screening. The Coast Guard then conducts enforcement based upon the law and regulation for mariners. When a mariner takes a drug test, the testing laboratory conducts a 5-panel screening to detect the use of marijuana, cocaine, opiates, phencyclidine (PCP) or amphetamines.

In the maritime enforcement business, it was normal to get 2 to 3 failures a month. The ones that always surprised me were the pre-employment tests.

The drug test was no surprise, yet they'd come up with a positive test and act as if they didn't know how that could possibly happen to them.

There was never a shortage of creative excuses for the positive drug test. One mariner told me he tested positive for cocaine because he had sex with a woman that took the drug. I explained that the drug test doesn't work that way, and I subsequently took his MMD away. Sometimes these rocket scientists would go out and buy off-the-shelf products to disguise their urine samples. Then, they could never explain why their urine had 1200% more phosphates than a normal living, breathing human being. Drug enforcement was, and still is the bulk of the caseload.

The average Coast Guard investigator handled 30 to 50 cases at any one time. Then Operation DRYDOCK came along. Over the next year, we dealt with mariners that somehow "forgot" about their assault with a deadly weapon, burglary, child molestation, drug, and rape or robbery convictions among many other such offenses, including their prison time. Many of the mariners referred to us had offenses that were years old and some were near the assessment periods. However, one case turned out to be a bit more serious.

Operation DRYDOCK referred two brothers to us for an investigation based upon their MMD application; Troy and his brother, Dino. Of the two, the only one I dealt with was Troy. His brother stayed under the radar and we never did have contact with him. Their story reads like something out of a crime story for dummies. Yet, Troy had enough sense and ability to plan; he just planned to live on the other side of the legal road.

Years before my encounter with Troy, both he and his brother were arrested in San Francisco with weapons and full body armor after an attempted robbery (and speculated intended killing) of a nightclub owner. For their crimes, both received convictions and were sentenced to spend time at California's maximum-security Pelican Bay prison.

While incarcerated, these two began a plan upon their release – they would obtain merchant documents and get employment in the maritime trade. Even though the requirement to receive the MMD was completion of approved training and proof of sea time, they would get around that.

Both brothers submitted MMD applications to the Coast Guard claiming they earned their sea time while living in Tuvalu, a small island in the Pacific. We never found any evidence that they ever stepped foot on the island, and their maritime experience proved to be fraudulent. Then there was the matter of the MMD application asking about prior convictions. Somehow, both brothers forgot the years they served in a maximum-security prison and claimed that they had clean records.

Even though submitting a false official statement on a government application is a criminal offense under 18 U.S. Code 1001, the chances of a successful conviction are slim. The United States Attorney is a politically appointed position and typically pursues high-profile cases. If the crime is a hot topic that will yield many years in prison or a hefty asset forfeiture; that will be their focus - not merchant mariners lying on an application. If a mariner failed to disclose a criminal history, the odds were good that no one would ever find out.

During the initial case against Troy and Dino, the evidence was certain to bring a conviction. Troy is a planner and I believe his next move was part of his roadmap to shorten their sentence. The brothers hired an attorney who apparently had issues himself. Their claim of attorney misconduct successfully made it through the appellate court, overturning their convictions. This didn't become apparent to us until a couple of interviews with him.

During our initial interview, Troy came into the office looking like he shopped for his clothes at "Gangs-R-Us." He looked like a tough character and it was no surprise that he was a prior Pelican Bay resident. A couple weeks later, we brought him in again for another interview.

By this time, I had voided his MMD and he was pursuing an appeal, claiming his racial status was under attack. Only now, he was well dressed and articulate. I almost didn't recognize him. At his side was his maritime union representative. Throughout the meeting, Troy was well spoken and professional. His union rep however, was another case. He rambled on incoherently referring to issues having nothing to do with the case we were pursuing. The meeting was getting completely out of hand and I finally asked Troy, "Do you really want this guy to represent you?" He just grinned and gave me a wink. I knew right then that this was his plan, to once again use poor representation to aid his cause.

To make matters worse, while pursuing cases against a steady flow of criminals, we also had to deal with a micromanaging structure above us. In a sense, we were "geographically challenged." The investigations department was located on the same facility as the Coast Guard District 11 staff. Other investigations offices had the luxury of being located away from the districts – they could work their cases without unneeded interference and second-guessing. While we were actively working the cases, the District would consistently inject opinion inconsistent with the law.

The D11 office staff continued to tell me that I was going too hard on Troy and he had served his time. In effect, I was picking on him and that he was actually a "nice guy trying to get his life together." They failed to remember the fraudulent application. Even with an overturned conviction, the law requires disclosure on the application. The D11 folks also failed to remember the part about how the brothers claimed maritime experience that they never earned on an island where they never lived. Sometimes our greatest challenges are not against criminals and terrorists; we fight against micromanaging fools in positions of power.

On Friday April 2, 2003, Troy came to the Coast Guard Regional Exam Center (REC) just downstairs from my office at the time. Fridays were always quiet in the REC. They were open only a half-day and there was a skeleton crew. I received an urgent call for help. Troy was in the office causing a ruckus and demanding the return of his MMD.

Since I had the document in my possession, I went downstairs to talk with him and calm the situation down. He wanted his MMD and claimed that I was after him because of his racial status. I explained that was not the case; I took his MMD because he failed to disclose his criminal background and claimed fraudulent sea time. I told him he should leave and not cause further problems for the women in the office. As he walked out the door, I wondered about his sudden urgency to get the MMD back. I was sure he chose Friday to intimidate the workers in the REC into getting what he wanted...but why now?

The answer came four days later. The news detailed a story about the robbery of a jewelry store in San Francisco. The culprits cut a hole into the wall of the adjoining store and waited for workers to arrive the next day. The robbers bound the employees and forced the manager to open the safe. The estimated take was $6 million in jewelry. The suspects were Troy and Dino. While I can't prove this, I believe Troy's plan was to use his access to the maritime nexus and fence the jewels overseas. The Operation DRYDOCK Task Force interfered with his plan.

Operation DRYDOCK reviewed over 220,000 merchant mariners. The result: Thousands of mariners were identified with possible fraud or other administrative issues, including some with active arrest warrants. Nine of those mariners appeared to have possible links to terrorism.

A Review

This chapter looked at the sailors. There are scores of mariners operating on the waters with long-distinguished careers. To be a professional mariner is a noble calling. They operate the passenger vessels that citizens rely on each day for safe travel. They work on cargo and tank ships moving hazardous materials along our coasts and rivers. They transport food supplies and vital cargoes that sustain our nation. They also move weapons and explosives needed to support our troops in wars that are not popular with terrorist elements.

Unfortunately, the profession also draws some for the wrong reasons. As we've seen earlier, the maritime industry is a place where those with criminal histories could attempt to turn their life around. For some, it is a safe place to hunt their victims and to hide. Others may find opportunity by moving illicit cargoes, while some engage in drug use. A staple of Coast Guard investigators departments is the enforcement of drug use by mariners. This maritime threat by the few outside the lines of the law presents a constant danger to our nation.

Chapter Seven

Barges and Towboats

Each type of vessel might have a specific use, or may have a wide variety of uses. Barges for instance may carry fuel, oil and dangerous caustic chemicals; dry cargo, construction and specialty equipment.

Given that, these vessels operate on different geographic routes depending upon their manufacture and the specific cargo they transport. Generally, aside from specialty barges, they transport cargo along ocean-going, coastwise or inland river routes.

As an example of size, typical inland river Dry Cargo barges are 35 feet wide, 200 feet long and have a 12-foot draft. Their weight is usually between 800 to 900 tons (empty). Dry Cargo barges can often carry 1500 tons of cargo. The capacity, physical size and weight are important factors regarding safe movement, as we will be see ahead.

Unlike many self-propelled vessels, moving barges from one port to another becomes a safety issue. Because of the large size and weight, it becomes an issue of restricted maneuverability. Barges are moved by a small towboat pushing from behind, towing from ahead or attached to the side by a series of lines and cables.

Other factors in the safe maneuverability of these expansive cargo loads are water currents, winds, loss of visibility due to environmental conditions and the minimum required forward speed, known as, "bare steerageway". In order for the rudder to effectively control direction and "steer" quickly, the vessel must maintain a minimum speed. Without bare steerageway, the vessel will quickly go out of control. Likewise, if the towboat experiences a mechanical failure, the multi-ton load becomes uncontrollable very quickly. Other vessels or infrastructure (locks, dams, bridges, piers, etc) are then in danger.

As an illustration of the maneuverability issues associated with barges and towboats (often referred to as a "tug & tow"), let's look at the Mississippi River. In the Upper Mississippi river north of St. Louis, barges are limited because of the dimension of the various river locks. There are 29 locks and dams maintained in the Upper Mississippi river region by the U.S. Army Corps of Engineers. Because of the lock width, barges moving along the northern portion of the river are restricted to a barge configuration of no more than 3-wide and 5-long. Given a 75-foot towboat, the entire length is nearly 1,100-feet long, pushing 22,500 tons of cargo.

Many of the locks in the Upper Mississippi river are 110-feet wide and 600-feet long. Given the 15-barge tow described above, a typical tow must push nine barges into the lock, then back out and wait for the first "cut" to be pulled through the locks by assist vehicles. Once the lock is clear, the remaining six barges and tow vessel enters the locks. Once through, the entire string of 15-barges is re-coupled and continues the transit. This procedure is slow and requires a great deal of skill by the Master of the tow vessel.

American Commercial Lines (ACL) is the second largest provider of dry and liquid cargo barges within the inland waterway systems of the United States. The company recently announced a plan to increase the cargo capacity of 30 barges in order to carry up to 30,000 barrels of liquid cargo.

According to ACL, moving a single barge is equivalent to the cargo within 15 rail cars or 80 trucks. Given this comparison, the potential explosive power or the potential for massive pollution incidents from specific cargoes is enormous.

When Things go Wrong

None of the following scenarios is the result of terrorism. This is a look at what could go wrong given the descriptive issues noted above that are related to barges and towboats. Many things could have been done differently. For some of the events listed below, the blame falls upon negligent operation, training shortfalls, equipment failure, environmental conditions, a physical inability to control a vessel by the operator, or a combination of many factors. The result of some of these incidents prompted regulatory changes; albeit very slow in some cases.

While maritime operators have attempted to take a proactive security posture, many holes continue to exist. Those shortfalls are not going to be specifically identified in this text. Some law enforcement and regulatory agencies are working hard to fill the gaps before our adversaries exploit them.

In the early morning hours of September 22, 1993, the pilot of the towboat, *Mauvilla* departed Mobile, Alabama and began a slow trek up the Mobile River pushing a string of barges. Blacked out by the fog, the pilot became disoriented and made a wrong turn. In this case, the operator of the *Mauvilla* was inexperienced on the radar – a skill certainly needed for the operation of a tug and tow in that environment. As the towboat pilot moved along in the darkness, he saw a line on his radar ahead of him and believed that the image was another towboat ahead of him. Intending to tie off to the other vessel, the "towboat" on his radar was the CSX rail bridge.

The National Transportation Safety Board (NTSB) investigation found the towboat *Mauvilla* struck the bridge causing a 38-inch misalignment of the track rails. The collision broke the barges free and the crew scrambled in the darkness to locate and re-lash the barges to the tug. They were completely unaware of the impending tragedy to occur moments later. The Amtrak Sunset Limited passenger train quickly approached at a speed of over 70 miles per hour. As the train passed through the broken rails, it was hurled through the darkness from the bridge and into the murky mud below killing 47 people.

This incident occurred in a remote area, slowing the ability of first responders to search for and recover victims. There is no way to know how many victims met their death waiting for help to arrive. As daylight appeared, the isolated area and devastation increased the shock value through the eye of the news camera. The CSX train bridge, like many around the country are located in isolated and often unattended areas. This is not a fault of anyone; this is a fact of rail infrastructure.

Aside from the regular maintenance to the bridge and rail systems, it is not possible to provide 24-hour monitoring. Rail providers have utilized new technologies to provide alerts when track rails are separated. Nevertheless, nothing can guarantee every bridge will be safe as long as heavy cargo vessels operate near them.

In the CSX bridge disaster, lives were lost and commerce was severely impacted. The incident made the bridge unusable. Recovery operations and the ensuing maritime casualty investigation continued for weeks. On average, over 2,500 CSX rail cars transit through the state of Alabama in a single week. After the accident, trains were redirected to other rail systems as they could be fit into existing track schedules. A conservative estimate of the overall cost of lives, damages, recovery and the economic consequence exceeded millions of dollars.

Another deadly event occurred in Oklahoma in May of 2002. During the early morning hours as commuters began their drive to work, the towboat *Robert Y. Love* pushing two empty tank barges collided with the Interstate 40 Bridge. The impact by the barges against the bridge support caused a 503-foot section of the elevated highway bridge to fall onto the barges below.

As traffic continued, eight passenger vehicles and three tractor-trailers descended to tragedy into the water and onto the portions of fallen bridge. In the end, 14 people fell to their deaths and five more were seriously injured. According to the NTSB investigation, the Master of the towboat had an abnormal heart rhythm causing unconsciousness as he neared the bridge.

The affected portion of the Interstate 40 Bridge near Webbers Falls, Oklahoma is a main thoroughfare for commuter traffic and ground freight. The waterway below is a common inland channel for maritime access and shipping. The overall economic costs to the bridge and barges exceeded $30 Million dollars. For months, traffic was diverted miles away to a nearby highway. Unlike the CSX Train Bridge incident, the Interstate 40 Bridge is well traveled and highly visible. Yet, both cases show location doesn't matter. Aside from regular preventative maintenance conducted on bridges, a constant security posture is not possible with thousands of rail and highway bridges in use throughout the nation.

U.S. Coast Guard statistics noted in the 2006 Marine Casualty and Pollution Database show there are over 31,900 barges operating in navigable waters of the U.S. Of those, most are general freight barges. Yet, there are almost 4,800 Tank barges transporting liquid cargoes, oil products and dangerous chemicals.

Many products carried via barge or tank ship are extremely dangerous and if released into the environment may destroy the eco-system or have deadly health effects on the populace if released into the atmosphere or water tables. In addition to common chemicals used for manufacturing, ammonia, benzene, cyanide, dioxins and pesticides move along our waterways each day. One of these chemicals, methyl isocyanate (MIC), is a chemical ingredient for the manufacture of adhesives and pesticide. In 1984, an accidental release of MIC enveloped the air around Bhopal, India killing thousands.

Accidents will happen. There is no current ability to prevent a multi-ton vessel from impacting bridges, waterside facilities or rail networks when things go wrong. According to the marine casualty statistics from the U.S. Coast Guard between 2003 and 2006, there were 3,383 and 3,065 marine casualties for freight and tank barges respectively.

As noted earlier in this chapter, barges rely upon the propulsion and steering of a towboat. When a mechanical failure occurs, the heavy-laden cargo quickly becomes an uncontrollable battering ram as seen above, and if carrying noxious chemicals, a threat to the environment and surrounding population.

Given the vital importance of the towboat in the movement of maritime cargo, a review of U.S. Coast Guard incident reports for the same 2003 to 2006 period shows there were 8,852 marine casualties. In an attempt to identify key causal factors of marine casualties, the data source used for the figures above failed to provide a level of specificity.

Given that, I then reviewed an earlier Coast Guard database of all marine casualties. The records used covered the same length of time, but different years. I looked at the period of 1998 to 2001. During the four-year period there were over 6,100 marine casualties citing a loss of vessel control. The following is an overview of causal factors during the 1998 to 2001 period:

- Propulsion loss: 64 percent.
- Steering loss: 23 Percent.
- Propulsion/Steering Combination: 11 Percent.
- Other factors: 2 percent.

As noted earlier, mechanical failures can propel a dangerous, heavy-laden freight or chemical barge into the path of disaster. Ironically, the majority of towing vessels operating within U.S. waters are not required to be inspected by the Coast Guard.

Towing vessels and operators are held to regulation for safe operation and navigation. However, unless the towing vessel operates on an international route, they are generally free from vessel inspections ensuring they are mechanically sound.

Barge Security

According to the facts provided earlier, there are over 31,900 barges operating within the U.S. When these barges are not in transit, being loaded or unloaded, many are left unattended. Often times, barges are moored at derelict piers, left in anchorage areas in harbors or bays and sometimes pushed ashore in low tide along rivers.

Even though Title 33 of the Code of Federal Regulations (CFR) defines specific security regulations for barges, the CFR says that an unmanned barge arriving at a chemical, oil or cargo facility does not require a Declaration of Security for the vessel.

Yet, some barges may carry explosives and tank barges may retain flammable or explosive amounts of liquid cargoes within the tanks. In 2003, the Coast Guard recognized the potential for an incident during an explosive loading operation in Washington State.

In order to protect the barge during the operation, they published a notice within the Federal Register defining a security and safety zone around the vessel.

According to the Coast Guard, the action was done to protect the barge from, "*sabotage, other subversive acts, or accidents*".

In addition to the barges noted above, there are many abandoned vessels along various U.S. waterways. When business is bad for barge operators and the cost of repairs or cleaning internal tanks from old product becomes an unmanageable expense, barges are abandoned. In effect, they become hazards to navigation and sometimes a toxic waste dump. Ironically, it is not against the law to abandon a vessel.

The owner is responsible for the cleanup of a pollution incident, yet many times the owner is bankrupt and unable to be identified. In this instance the Comprehensive Environmental Response, Compensation Liability Act (CERCLA) of 1980 takes over and the cleanup cost often reaches into the millions. Funding through the CERCLA Hazardous Substance Superfund in the end becomes an expense for the taxpayer.

A Review

In this section, we have touched upon a few areas where barges and their accompanying tow vessels can have a deadly impact if not carefully monitored and inspected. We have seen how the gross weight and motion of a large cargo-laden vessel can easily wipe out vital infrastructure, kill and leave vast economic repercussions. As the two bridge incidents show, location does not matter and monitoring each vessel or bridge is not feasible.

We have seen that on any given day there are generally millions of tons of liquid cargoes, oil products and dangerous chemicals moving along

U.S. navigable waterways by barge. Many cargoes are corrosives, poisons, flammable or explosive substances.

As they stealthily travel along waterways in the midst of densely populated regions, they offer the frightening potential to injure or kill if their cargo releases into the atmosphere. Some would likely cause serious effects upon our environment and our drinking water.

Some vessel security issues were discussed regarding barges, holes in security regulations and the ability to easily abandon them leaving a costly safety, environmental and economic impact. One question I frequently hear when discussing this book is, *"Aren't you going to be showing the terrorist how to attack us?"* Given that, numerous issues were not discussed in this text, as I do not intend to make this a, "How-to" book for the terrorist.

Realistically, a terrorist group does not need my help finding vulnerable areas. For years, much of our vital infrastructure and potentially sensitive information was clearly displayed on the Internet for all to see. Various raids against terror groups around the globe verify that fact.

Not until we were attacked on 9/11 did we begin to wake up and realize we are not untouchable. Even so, while we have taken steps to protect our infrastructure by taking information off the web, it is still available in many places. Even worse are the organizations within our own country that, in the name of free information, go out of their way to publish images and sensitive materials that could later be used to kill us. Given the info presented, what prevents the thousands of barges operating throughout our nation from becoming a safety and security threat?

A common theme will be seen in the pages ahead as we explore various types of vessels and their potential to be used against us by our adversaries. As we've seen, we can't be everywhere at all times to prevent an incident. Many incidents that have been thwarted were the result of good police work, sometimes through shared intelligence and often times by luck.

The premise here is that the Maritime Transportation System may be used as a weapon by an adversary; thus the overview of the vessels and some history. In order to prevent a weapon from being used against you it is vital to understand how it can be used and what indicators exist, allowing you the opportunity to do something about it before the strike.

Chapter Eight

Freight and Tank Ships

The "Barge and Towboats" chapter illustrated how multi-ton loads of fuel, oils and caustic cargoes can impact waterways and threaten the safety of populated areas.

Tank ships likewise carry dangerous cargoes but in much larger quantities and therefore become much easier targets. In an earlier chapter, we discussed how the line between criminal acts and terrorist incidents are often transparent. This chapter deals with a variety of different types of cargo carriers and discusses historical incidents affecting the safety and security of the maritime nexus.

Maritime shipping is the most cost efficient mechanism for the transport of cargo. In many cases, it is the only feasible option because of the volume and size of some products. For tank ships carrying thousands of barrels of oils, chemicals or other liquids internationally, there is no other way. A container ship carrying hundreds of 40-foot containers would require nearly the equivalent amount of cargo aircraft to transport the same payload. Large equipment and oversized structures manufactured in one geographic location is often shipped to the final destination in other parts of the globe.

Years ago, the city of Oakland, California contracted the manufacture and delivery of large gantry cranes for the shipping port. The large, "Super Paramax Cranes" were designed and built in Shanghai, China. After a lengthy construction period, these huge cranes were loaded aboard ships for the long trans-Pacific voyage.

Timing the initial transit into the San Francisco Bay was crucial since the cranes were so large. At the entrance to the bay stands the Golden Gate Bridge. The bridge typically has a clearance of 220 feet. Even so, movement occurred at low tide and the ship had to fill the ballast tanks so the vessel would be heavier and ride lower, allowing the cranes to clear the bridge.

Considering the clearance and preparation needed, you can see the maritime route was the only viable option for delivery other than building the cranes on site. The construction area needed would encompass a large portion of a thriving shipping port, eliminating a large segment of the annual cargo and container shipping. This option would cost the port, the city and supporting industries millions in financial losses. This one example shows that maritime shipping is sometimes the only option and economically the best alternative pound for pound of cargo.

Given the financially viable benefit of maritime cargo noted above, this vital transportation avenue is an easy targeting opportunity for terrorists. While cargo ships are vulnerable to attack, many threats may not be recognized until the last moments prior to an assault. Additionally, response time by law enforcement and security forces often fail to circumvent the incident. Even more so, isolated vessels at sea face greater susceptibility, as response options are even less effective. Terror groups may act because of political, religious, social reasons or any number of triggers may drive them.

Regardless of the reason, there is always a target and a terrorist will always find a rationalization to their actions. In the case of the February 1998 Fatwa by Usama bin Laden, all *"Americans and their allies--civilians and military"* are targets. For another group the focus of their resentment may be a specific corporation, shipping firm or country doing business with the U.S. or western interests. Still other terrorist factions might focus their actions against local governments or an ethnic populace. An attack against a ship moving cargo influences the economic base of the region, in a sense, hitting their target.

There is a misconception that maritime attacks by terrorists require significant expense and sophistication. This is a falsity. Aside from attacks requiring detailed knowledge of explosives, many attacks can be done using common weaponry, or sometimes none at all. A small vessel can impede maneuvering of a larger cargo ship causing grounding, impact with bridges or infrastructure and possibly an oil spill. In either case, the vessel movement ceases and the ship is potentially damaged.

Everyday, large tank ships enter the coastal waters of the United States. In strategic areas in the Gulf of Mexico, offshore lightering areas offload supertankers from overseas locations. These lightering areas prevent the need for large supertankers to transit up the Mississippi River. Because of the constant flow of mud, water and silt down the river, some areas are susceptible to vessel grounding. Other areas have strong currents near river bends, making safe navigation very difficult for the larger tank ships.

An attack on this type could cause a massive pollution incident, wreak havoc upon the environment, commerce and divert valuable resources. For years afterward, the fishing trade and supporting industries pay the price with lost revenue. The overall response operation runs into the millions of dollars.

When the Coast Guard reacts to a large-scale environmental incident, security patrols and response capabilities are minimized. During the March 1989 Valdez oil spill, I was assigned to the Coast Guard Cutter Morgenthau. We were just completing a hectic 90-day winter patrol in the Bering Sea when the Exxon Valdez ran aground. Instead of returning to our homeport, we stayed in the oil and coordinated additional maritime resources until another Cutter relieved us.

During the initial response and cleanup, Coast Guard vessels were diverted to this incident. In effect, drug, illegal migration, fisheries conservation and security patrols were curtailed. I saw the same thing occur at both the Haitian Exodus and TWA-800 incidents. Resources are flooded in the direction of the latest incident.

Is that wrong? No. It does however emphasize that Coast Guard resources are slim and they typically fail to have adequate backing for personnel and vessels until it becomes a political hot button. This is one area I will repeat throughout this book: When resources are diverted because of an incident, personnel and assets may become targets of a secondary attack. Other mission areas go unguarded.

In November 2000, The *Westchester*, an 800-foot Liberian tank ship spilled 554,400 gallons of crude oil in the Mississippi River after an apparent loss of power and subsequent grounding. Once again, the Coast Guard refocused their attention from other mission areas; 26-miles of river and the closure of two sets of locks to shipping traffic. The response required additional assets and 30 ships came to respond.

The Mississippi River is a major shipping route supporting the flow of commerce for the United States. I am not attempting to link negligent ship operation in Alaska or the grounding in Louisiana with terrorist activity. The point however, is that terrorist organizations use prior events as a guide for future operations. History shows that rogue regimes have no concern for environmental protection.

During the Gulf War of 1990, Suddam Hussein ordered the destruction of hundreds of oil wells in Kuwait. The result inflicted economic damage and diverted resources away from the area of battle. This kind of mindset was irrational knowing the environmental result. Yet, the terrorist sometimes cares more for the cause than the aftermath. The Occupational Health and Safety Administration (OSHA) recognizing the potential of hazardous environments resulting from terrorist attacks developed the Evacuation Planning Matrix. The guidance for this report, states: "As a nation, our understanding of the risk of terrorist releases and the agents involved continues to evolve." Given this understanding, it is vital that we recognize the potential of a maritime related spill as both an economic attack and diversion of resources precipitating the potential for subsequent acts.

Navigation and the Potential for Catastrophe

Years ago as a marine investigator in the San Francisco Bay area, I had a near-catastrophic case. A local fisherman in a small boat was in the path of an oncoming container ship. According to the International Navigation rule 9, *"A vessel of less than 20 meters in length or a sailing vessel shall not impede the passage of a vessel which can safely navigate only within a narrow channel or fairway."* Given the maritime regulations, the container ship had the right of way. Nevertheless, instead of maneuvering out of the path of the larger ship, the fisherman remained in place. In response, the Harbor Pilot sounded the horn warning of a possible collision.

Given the narrow channel where the larger ship had to maneuver, the fisherman should have yielded to the larger vessel. Yet, he stayed in place and threw his nets in front of the oncoming ship. The Harbor Pilot had only two choices: run the fisherman over, or pull the ship's engines at "All Stop" and then into reverse. In this case, the container ship had a single screw propeller. The effect of reversing a large vessel with a single screw tends to cause the stern of the ship to turn.

As the Harbor Pilot worked to avoid a collision and maintain control of the vessel, the ship was now in danger of backing into the Oakland Bay Bridge during rush-hour traffic. In a last ditch effort to prevent a new collision scenario with the bridge and a possible mass-casualty, the Harbor Pilot dropped the anchor, narrowly averting catastrophe. Civil penalty action was later taken against the fisherman.

This is just one example of how a small boat in a narrow channel can influence the maneuverability of larger vessels and cause disaster. The whole incident occurred within just a few minutes. Even the best response time by maritime security forces would have no effect.

Imagine the aftermath of such an incident. Had the container ship collided with the bridge precipitating a collapse, there certainly would be scores of horrific deaths and injuries to commuters traveling across the span. Both inbound and outbound commercial vessel traffic would cease. The response, rescue and recovery of victims would take days or weeks. The closure of a vital transportation artery, excavation and reconstruction would cost millions.

An incident of this magnitude resides as a top news story for weeks with commuters forced to find alternative transportation routes. Sometimes the lack of effective transportation infrastructure alternatives leaves commuters traveling on avenues not prepared for the increased volume of traffic. The resulting pandemonium and expense fits nicely into the goals of many terror groups. With little effort, a group could precipitate fear, death, confusion and a large economic calamity, coupled with worldwide news coverage.

The episode noted earlier with the fishing boat and the container ship reiterates my earlier assertion: There is no need for great expense and complexity to cause havoc to maritime shipping. A person with sophistication and expensive equipment did not cause this incident; it was an idiot with a small boat and a fishing net.

A Story of Two Bridges

While this chapter addresses maritime attacks

by terror groups, it is important to look at the cost of two recent episodes involving bridges near navigable waterways.

When the I-35W Bridge in Minneapolis, Minnesota collapsed on August 1, 2007, 13 people died and scores of others were injured. A cargo ship like the one in San Francisco did not collide with the bridge, nor is there any suggestion that this was an intended attack. It only serves as a comparison to describe the overall cost of such an event.

Shortly after the Minneapolis incident, I contacted the Coast Guard Public Affairs Officer (PAO) asking for the impact to commercial maritime commerce. The bridge collapse subsequently closed nine miles of the Mississippi River to commercial vessel traffic and began to have an immediate effect on the local economy. The Coast Guard spokesperson detailed how the incident stopped vessel traffic and cargo movement throughout the area. The PAO described the layoff of industry workers because of the collapse. With the waterway closed, mariners and the supporting industry of marine services felt an economic blow.

On November 7, 2007, the *Cosco Busan* struck the Oakland Bay Bridge cutting a 100-foot gash into the side of the ship. Had there been a direct impact with the bridge structure rather than a glancing blow to the bridge fender system, there may have been a mass-casualty scenario. Even so, the resulting 58,000-gallon oil spill diverted resources, damaged the environment and cost over $61 million.

The response to this incident proved to be a failure of communication between internal Coast Guard units. As a prior civilian investigator with the

Coast Guard in San Francisco, we operated under the control of the Marine Safety Office. Historically, Marine Safety Offices and operational units in the Coast Guard speak a different language. The maritime safety world is quite different from the operational side of the Coast Guard.

As I was preparing to leave for another position, Coast Guard commands prepared for a transition toward a Sector Command structure. The intent of the merger was to bring operational surface, aviation and marine safety units together under the same command allowing a, "Big picture" view of an incident for response.

There is a lot of value for a Commander to have a coordinated control of assets and response. Unfortunately, according to my discussions with Coast Guard personnel close to the investigation, when the *Cosco Busan* struck the bridge, operational personnel didn't understand the marine safety terminology or the magnitude of the event. The resulting response was inadequate.

During research for this book, I have found some writers declare that terrorist groups do not operate near shipping ports, along coastlines or in the proximity to maritime infrastructure. Why is that? Only a fool will attempt to predetermine what a terrorist will or will not do. It is like assuming that terrorists would never use aircraft as a weapon against buildings because they are afraid to fly. Everyday millions of tons of cargo transit through maritime ports worldwide. If a terrorist group stops cargo from moving, they succeed because maritime commerce is impacted.

In June of 2006, a threatening note was found

onboard the 30,000 ton refrigerated cargo ship, *Wild Lotus* in Port Hueneme, California. The harbor is the only deep-water seaport situated between Los Angeles and San Francisco. Cargo entering this location then transfers via rail or truck for final delivery. While nothing came of the threat, maritime shipping and follow-on intermodal commerce ceased while law enforcement investigated the incident.

Returning to a discussion from an earlier chapter, there is often a transparency between terrorist incidents and criminal events. Given that, terrorist groups learn and adapt from the transnational methodologies of drug smugglers and human traffickers. For years, smuggling operations utilized parasitic containers attached to ships as a means to transport drugs. These pods, when attached to larger cargo ships have little drag on vessel movement or stability and therefore, often go unnoticed. Given that, a terrorist could certainly use the same method as a delivery system for an explosive device or transfer of WMD.

The Australian Customs Service began purchasing remotely operated vehicles (ROV) for underwater inspections of cargo vessels shortly after the discovery of a large haul of cocaine onboard a South American ship. The cache valuing approximately $6 million entered the country in metal containers attached to the hull.

In 2004, smugglers from Venezuela stashed over $14 million worth of cocaine within the sea chest (the ship's underwater cooling port) of the Canadian ship, *Sheila Ann*. As far back as 1996, the Government Accountability Office reported that both Department of Defense and U.S. Coast Guard personnel were facing issues with parasitic containers attached to hulls of ships for drug smuggling. The report declared that some vessels were not inspected because they were carrying perishable cargo. No one wants to hold up a vessel at sea, board and search it and then cause cargo to spoil, especially if no contraband is found.

The use of ROV's or divers may be a viable option while a vessel is in port, but not for an at-sea inspection. There are a number of safety requirements for a subsurface inspection below a ship. There can be no operation of the rudder, propeller, sonar or depth measuring equipment. All intake suction used to cool the engines must cease. This equipment, if not controlled could kill or injure a diver or damage an ROV. In effect, the vessel will be dead in the water with no maneuvering capability while adrift in the open ocean.

At-sea inspections of vessels are thorough. Coast Guard boarding team members ensure full space accountability of every possible hidden compartment. Yet, the teams will not compromise safety of navigation and the condition of the vessel during a boarding. Given that, the hull of a ship is free game to a smuggler or terrorist. If a parasitic device contained an explosive device, chances are, no one will know until after it went off in a port or a vital navigable shipping channel.

In July 2000, the U.S. Customs Service (now Customs and Border Protection) seized 240 pounds of cocaine hidden inside the rudder trunk area. The area is large enough to hide not only drugs, but also illegal migrants seeking to enter the country. The International Maritime Organization published an information bulletin in December 2007 describing numerous accounts of migrant stowaways hiding within the rudder area.

This is not a new problem. In 1991, two stowaways bringing over $4 million in cocaine from Colombia were discovered within the rudder area of a tank ship entering New York. To be fair, it is important to note that not all migration efforts end well. Several migrants attempting to enter the country perish during their transit due to hypothermia, drowning, being pulled into the propeller suction or any number of ways due to the environment they place themselves in.

Given these scenarios, we can see there has been a long-term capability to bring drugs, people or weapons into the country by this often overlooked area on cargo ships. The examples noted above also indicate that the unscrupulous often have free access to vessels in foreign ports where security procedures are lax. Since 9/11, specific reporting and screening procedures implemented the 96-hour Advance Notice of Arrival. This allows Coast Guard and other intelligence personnel an opportunity to research and make judgments of the best vessels to inspect prior to entering port.

Even so, sometimes the best intelligence can miss things. There are current off-the-shelf technologies available that allow a terrorist to set off an explosive device from a distance. These attacks have occurred over and over again during the Iraq war against U.S. and coalition forces.

Earlier we looked at vessel maneuverability issues near bridges. If a strategically placed explosive device could damage steering capabilities, a ship approaching a bridge or other vital infrastructure could have a devastating effect. The following is just one example.

One bridge near a California port spans a navigational channel for cargo ships. Because the bridge height is low, the center span lifts allowing ships to pass. At other times, the bridge is equipped with both a rail system and a roadway. If this important transportation conduit were targeted, maritime, trucking and rail cargo movement would cease in addition to commuter traffic. While the design and placement of the bridge seems to be a sensible link to strategic regions, it also becomes a potential vulnerability.

Detection and targeting amongst the hundreds of ships entering ports each day becomes very difficult unless there is a solid tip-off regarding a specific vessel. We need to adopt a combination of shipboard detection, underwater inspections and increased security assets to ensure ships safely enter our ports. Even then, we face an enormity of challenges.

Throughout this chapter, we have addressed the economic value of maritime shipping compared to other transportation methods. We invalidated the myth that terror attacks require significant expense and sophistication. Obstructing safe navigation of large cargo vessels in narrow channels can damage our nation's vital infrastructure, potentially cause large environmental disasters and place citizens at risk. When a terror group effectively upsets the economy, they in fact succeed in hitting their target. We have also looked at the methods used by trans-national criminal groups and see that the same methods provide useful planning guides for the terrorist.

Finally, we see that with even the best intelligence and law enforcement capability, technology and the comprehensive range of issues within the maritime nexus can sometimes play against us. We need to increase our number of trained security personnel with knowledge of the maritime environment. We have seen in the *Cosco Busan* incident that maritime issues are sometimes different from other operational issues. Often times, instinct from the human element yields better results.

Chapter Nine

Small Boat Attacks and Security Forces

Every day, large tank ships enter the navigable waters of the United States. In strategic areas like the Gulf of Mexico, offshore lightering areas unload supertankers from around the globe. An attack on this type of platform causing a pollution incident could wreak havoc upon the environment, commerce and divert valuable resources.

On October 6, 2002, such an attack occurred against a tank ship when a small fishing boat packed with explosives rammed the French tanker *MV Limburg* off the coast of Yemen. The explosion caused the spill of 90,000 barrels of oil into the Gulf of Aden, killing one crewman and polluting 45-miles of coastline. A claim of responsibility initially came from the Aden-Abyan Islamic Army, suspected of association with Al-Qaeda. The same group earlier claimed responsibility for the October 2000 attack on the *USS Cole* killing 17 sailors and injuring 39 others. In the case of the USS Cole, there was a security presence onboard. Yet, the small boat gave no appearance of being a threat until it was too late. In both cases, terrorists attacked their targets in faster, more maneuverable vessels, all the while virtually unimpeded by potential security forces.

It is nearly impossible to have adequate maritime security forces for the protection of every ship operating near significant ports. Law enforcement budgets generally focus resources to protect citizens on the streets and little is offered to marine safety, security and response.

Years ago, cities in Northern California were facing budget issues. As a result, the funds needed for fireboats in Oakland and San Francisco would not be available or severely limited. This choice prevents any useful response capability if there were an attack against shipping in an area reliant upon petroleum facilities and ports. This was a bad idea. Marine police patrols are commonly minimally manned and have few resources. Cities expect the Coast Guard to be the, "Mother hen" of the ports.

Shortly after 9/11, I was the Intelligence Chief with the Coast Guard Marine Safety Office in Mobile, Alabama. We recognized that our resources were limited and I embarked upon building partnerships to share information (as we could) with security managers of waterside facilities. Through the partnership, they would report suspicious incidents to the Coast Guard. This process allowed us to have numerous eyes and ears reporting for us. The value of their reporting is that it came from personnel that live and work near the water. If something is amiss, they will recognize it and the source of the reporting was often very reliable. The reports were then forwarded up the chain to allow a broad comparison of incidents across the nation.

I met regularly with the security managers of

these facilities to discuss reporting and listen to their concerns. Many representatives from large chemical facilities voiced their opinion that the Coast Guard is responsible to protect their waterside operations. In fact, it is not a Coast Guard responsibility to provide security services for a business. This is the responsibility of the facility owners and operators themselves. The Coast Guard has responsibility to ensure that navigable waterways are safe. Coast Guard security personnel patrolled being mindful of suspicious incidents, but they also ensured safety of navigation on the waterways. Most security managers understood this was a viable business responsibility of theirs, although, some didn't see it that way. This was a case where they wanted to shoot me as the messenger.

Maritime security forces cannot be everywhere protecting every possible scenario. There are countless opportunities for a terror attack against vessels anywhere in the world. This is not the, "feel good" safety message people want to hear, but this is the reality. In fact, if we had a full complement of security forces to protect every ship, facility and shipping port, some would cry there is too much government intervention.

Additionally, the rules of engagement are often not clear for those expected to protect the waterways. If Coast Guard or local law enforcement maritime patrols recognized a potential incident, there could be a delay in response time simply because of the permissions needed to fire upon a small private vessel heading toward a cargo ship. We live in a world where law enforcement is second-guessed at every incident involving force. Civil liberty groups sometimes do more to protect our adversaries than allow our own personnel to protect our citizens. This environment inherently brings about a potential delay of action for the responder.

Maritime terror events require responders to quickly arrive to the aid of the attacked ship. An event like the *USS Cole* or *MV Limburg* could quickly become a trap for response vessels arriving to the scene. Ideally, incident planning should have occurred long before an attack. Air and surface exclusion areas must be set in place right away. It is vital that during the response, effective communication systems are set in place to prevent response personnel from becoming targets of a secondary attack. A diversion of resources is a simple method to disperse responders. Command personnel should know where everyone else is and have a view of the big picture, recognizing that their response could in fact leave other vital targets unguarded.

The Tamil Tigers

The Liberation Tigers of Tamil Eelam (LTTE), a terrorist group operating near Sri Lanka has shown a maritime capability to attack at will through small boat attacks. The group, known as the Tamil Tigers, began an effective maritime component in 1984. For years, the LTTE's, "Sea Tigers" have conducted successful small boat attacks against both the Sri Lankan Navy and commercial vessels in the region. Their area of operations is constantly monitored for potential attacks and even with security forces present, successful raids continue.

A common tactic of the Sea Tigers is a suicide attack. Such was the case of an assault that took place in October 2001. The LTTE attacked and destroyed the *MT Silk Pride*, an oil tanker carrying

650 metric tons of diesel and kerosene fuel. The attack killed four Sri Lankan Naval personnel and three Sea Tigers. The LTTE frequently sends multiple vessels toward their target in a "Swarm" formation, attacking from different directions. Often times, in the midst of the swarm comes a suicide boat.

In May 2006, the *MV Pearl Cruiser II* was carrying 710 security personnel and supplies. The *Pearl Cruiser II* is a merchant vessel used by the Sri Lankan Navy to transport personnel and supplies. On the day of the incident, the ship was under escort of a naval flotilla protected by six fast attack craft and a gunboat. Yet, the Sea Tigers still attacked.

The Sea Tigers approached in 18 boats armed with 20mm, 23mm and .50 caliber guns. As they began their swarm attack, the *Pearl Cruiser II* was virtually unprotected while the navy attempted to ward off the attack. With Sri Lankan naval forces in the fight, the *Pearl Cruiser II* was left alone and vulnerable. Six LTTE boats were loaded with explosives and operated by the, "Black Tigers." They are the maritime suicide branch. They could have easily sunk the vessel but opted not to do so. One of the naval vessels and the *Pearl Cruiser II* were flying the flag of the Sri Lankan Monitoring Mission (SLMM). Each vessel carried Scandinavian cease fire personnel onboard as part of the Cease-Fire Agreement (CFA) between the two forces. Speculation continues whether the LTTE chose not to sink the ship because of the monitors or, whether they intended to seize the vessel and crew. While both the LTTE and Sri Lankan forces were engaged in the fight, the *Pearl Cruiser II* made a run for Indian waters, avoiding the attack. In the end, the LTTE lost 5 Sea Tiger boats and an estimated 50 personnel. The Sri Lankan Navy lost 1 vessel and 17 sailors.

Security Forces in the U.S. are rarely capable to thwart an LTTE-type attack on vessels. As noted earlier, maritime security and law enforcement forces are minimally manned. Those that are in operation are functioning in port security and vessel escort roles. Coast Guard Marine Safety and Security Teams (MSST) may have vessels in operation and others on standby. Yet, if they were escorting high interest vessels carrying dangerous cargoes, they would be hard pressed to break off and respond to an offshore attack.

The entire *Pearl Cruiser II* incident occurred within a 90-minute period. By the time additional MSST units were to arrive on scene, the attack could be done. In the LTTE attack noted above, the Sri Lankan Navy eventually had helicopter support. Even so, if the Sea Tigers were going to sink the *Pearl Cruiser II*, even a helicopter would have little effect. Our MSST personnel would most likely benefit from joint tactics training with units like the Sri Lankan Navy that face hostile issues each day.

Our Coast Guard units need more vessels and trained crews. Unfortunately, instead of declaring operational limitations to obtain more resources, commanders tend to place additional duties upon those presently serving. After all, the Coast Guard always pulls through. In the last few years, the service is starting to get better at recognizing fatigue issues to protect their personnel. Congress needs to provide adequate funding for maritime security. It is unrealistic to expect a small service like the Coast Guard to conduct worldwide missions and protect 361 U.S. maritime ports with a force smaller than the New York City Police force.

In this chapter, we've seen that terrorist elements can attack maritime targets at will using smaller boats that are more maneuverable, often times without intervention by security forces. When law enforcement budgets are tight, maritime security resources that are already slim, get cut further. Politicians understand that the maritime arena is both important and vulnerable. However, they don't understand the complexities of the issue and do little to ensure adequate resources exist. For a time, many corporations operating at waterside facilities misconceived the responsibilities of the Coast Guard. The belief was that maritime security is a sole Coast Guard problem and felt they were exempt from providing security for their own facilities.

Traditionally, the Coast Guard operates underfunded and undermanned. The service only gets worthy attention and funding during a crisis like the Valdez spill, the Midwest floods of the 1990's, the Haitian Exodus, TWA-800 or Hurricane Katrina. It's unfortunate that tragedy must come before the service is funded to do the jobs everyone expects of them.

With the formation of the Department of Homeland Security, waterside facilities are now assisted with port security grants. This initiative causes facility owners to take a good look at their own security posture and comply with updated regulation. While the grants help fund initiatives allowing greater protection to the facilities, some areas are still vulnerable from the perspective of a waterside attack.

A positive initiative was the formation of Area Maritime Security Committees in various ports around the country. Members of the committees represent maritime shipping corporations, law enforcement and Coast Guard. There is more often than not an interesting dynamic among the membership of the committee. Corporate maritime personnel have an expectation of law enforcement and the Coast Guard to protect them when in fact these commercial enterprises hold the keys to political ears. They sometimes have a greater chance of getting things done than the regulatory bodies.

In this chapter, we've seen there are potential issues for use of force and an effective response to an incident. Finally, the Tamil Tigers show that small boats can be an effective aggressor and do harm to larger vessels, often times at will.

Chapter Ten

The Pirates

Earlier, we saw that terrorist elements seek to target both U.S. and Western Allies. Ships from these allied countries are unprotected as they operate throughout the world. In today's Internet environment, a terrorist can develop a targeting plan and track a vessel online. Depending upon the vessel tracking service, they can identify the vessel name, country, shipping company, last port of call, next port of call, predicted arrival date, and sometimes, the type of cargo.

Since the 9/11 attacks, whenever there is a significant terror attack anywhere in the world, we hear about it on the news. Yet, when pirates attack, very little is mentioned and it goes unnoticed unless the scenario makes for a good news story. Even so, like today's terrorist, pirates are organized. They too utilize current communications technologies and benefit from an organized logistics and support chain. In effect, they are the mafia of the water.

Pirates attack vessels in isolated shipping areas throughout the world. Their maritime raids impact worldwide economies, seizing control of vessels as they move cargo around the globe. In the chapter on freight ships, we saw that moving cargo by sea is the best economic alternative for international shipping. Yet, as pirates continue their unhindered operations, maritime transport companies become hesitant to operate in the area. Looking back over a 10-year period during 1995 to 2006, there were 2,521 instances where pirates boarded vessels worldwide.

While air cargo offers timely delivery, the cost is many times insurmountable. According to the International Chamber of Commerce (ICC) Commercial Crime Services, significant numbers of attacks occur in South East Asia, the Indian Sub Continent, Africa, the Red Sea, the Arabian Sea, South and Central America and in the Caribbean.

In one of those areas in South East Asia, the Malacca Straits is one of the busiest shipping lanes in the world. Over 50,000 vessels pass through the area each year. Historically, the Malacca Straits is known for frequent incidents of piracy. The US Energy Information Administration describes it as a "World Oil Chokepoint" moving approximately 15 million barrels of oil through the straits each day. The narrow channel is a vital link between the Indian Ocean to the South China Sea and Pacific Oceans. Imagine the effects if an attack against a supertanker caused a spill. The Exxon Valdez incident on March 24, 1989, poured 240,000 barrels into the sea and took six months to cleanup. Such an impact to a vital shipping route like the Malacca Straits would result in dire global consequences.

This is the type of region terror organizations like Al-Qaeda use to practice their surveillance and tactical operations. In fact, U.S. Troops found videos in an Al-Qaeda hideout in Afghanistan showing Malaysian boats on patrol in the straits. The evidence can only indicate their intention to target this aspect of the Marine Transportation System. As multi-national collaboration developed to attack the problem, piracy incidents began to decline since 2004. Even so, given the strategic location for international shipping, this area should not be overlooked.

Generally, pirate attacks against ships in Asia are intended for robbery. Many assaults occur during late night or early morning hours when the vessel is at anchorage or moored. Robbers board the vessel, steal what they can and depart unnoticed. In some cases, robbers opened specific cargo containers, indicating the possibility that they have had access to the vessel or are in collusion with others having shipping and cargo information. At other times, armed pirates attempted to intercept the vessel in small boats transiting through the Malacca Straits or along coastal areas. Fortunately, in some cases, alert crews successfully averted pirate attacks because of keen observation, alarms and anti-piracy measures.

Another more dangerous aspect of pirate attacks is a hijacking. In April 1998, the *Petro Ranger*, a tank ship hauling diesel and jet fuel came under attack. The ship was heading for Vietnam when a dozen pirates climbed onboard armed with machetes and guns. In short order, the pirates bound the crew of 20 and held them as prisoners for 13 days. The captors then painted and renamed the ship to read *MV Wilby* and set a course toward Hainan Island. Days later, two tank ships arrived and offloaded nearly $3 million worth of cargo.

The story of the vessel continued to get worse. Chinese patrols boarded the ship, and convinced the crew was engaged in smuggling, took them into custody and seized the vessel. In the end, the crew was released and the ship returned after the owners paid a fine. The stolen cargo was never found.

In July 2006, pirates approached and boarded

the *Bintang Samudra,* transiting through the Straits. Unlike typical attacks, this occurred in the morning daylight hours. The pirates, dressed in military fatigues, were armed with automatic weapons and grenade launchers. They demanded and received money from the master prior to leaving. The pirates then claimed they were associated with the Free Aceh Movement (GAM), a known terrorist group operating in the area.

While there are frequent claims of association with GAM, speculation continues why the pirates boarded the vessel during daylight hours and departed with nothing more than cash. Another issue is the amount of armament carried during the incident. Other incidents where pirates carried weapons of this nature were related to kidnappings for ransom. Perhaps the *Bintang Samudra* was incorrectly targeted.

An Increase of African Piracy Attacks

The IMB reports that 2007 was an active year with an overall increase of piracy by ten percent. Violent attacks against crewman increased by 35 percent. The heightened number of piracy incidents is primarily due to attacks in both Nigeria and Somalia. Both countries face political disorder and have neither the ability nor the will to counter organized crime groups attacking vessels in the region. Incidents of piracy off the coast of Somalia are directly proportional to the political environment.

During the summer of 2006, the Union of Islamic Courts (UIC) came to power in Somalia. Immediately afterward, the UIC announced that they would punish those engaged in piracy according to Sharia law.

For a time the incidents ceased, until they struck the United Arab Emirates cargo ship, *MV Veesham I*. A small boat with six pirates boarded and took control of the cargo ship shortly after leaving port. Initially the pirates demanded a $1 million ransom; negotiations lowered the amount to $150,000. The UIC in response, set to sea in small boats, recaptured the vessel and rescued the crew after a gun battle with the pirates. The UIC withstood the challenge to their authority.

Unfortunately, the success was short-lived. One month later, Ethiopian forces entered Somalia gaining political control of the country. They pushed the UIC out of power. With the UIC gone, the organized gangs of pirates no longer feared governmental retribution for their offshore attacks. Offshore piracy assaults continued again.

Somali pirates operate with impunity hundreds of miles off the coast and they typically attack in small, high-powered boats capable of out-maneuvering larger cargo ships. Because of the distance they travel for their attacks, it is evident that they have an organized logistical network. After leaving my investigations position years ago, I went back to work in the intelligence business. Nearly every day, we focused on a new drug smuggling case. Like the small Somali pirate boats, drug runners operate fast, high-powered, low profile boats. To successfully transit the long routes needed to import their drugs, they rely on pre-positioned vessels acting as lookouts for law enforcement. Additionally, they are a refueling platform. Somali pirates have a similar network.

Somali pirates often board vessels wearing fatigues carrying military-style weapons, specialized GPS and communications systems. Once onboard, they quickly seize control of the vessel and begin stealing cargo, shipboard electronics equipment and personal items and money from the crew. In several instances, ships attempted to out run the pirates; few succeeded. Yet, with the Somalis' faster boats, the attempt is often pointless. Aiming a Rocket Propelled Grenade (RPG) at the vessel, they order the ship to stop.

Even though the cargo ship is much larger than the pirate boat, just a few sailors operate them. If attacked by an RPG, the ship becomes vulnerable to fire and that's one thing no sailor wants. If a ship burns, there's nowhere to go. When combating a fire, the ship must stop or else the prevailing wind caused by forward motion of the vessel feeds the fire, making matters worse. The Captain generally has two choices: risk catastrophic damage to the vessel, risk crew safety and stop, or, protect the ship and stop. A minimal crew with no security protection stands little chance of successfully fighting a fire and out maneuvering a smaller, faster boat armed with weapons. The ship will always stop and the pirates know that.

Pirates hold crews hostage in exchange for a ransom, sometimes for months at a time. During nation's6, there were 87 hostages taken during Somali piracy incidents. In May 2007, Somali pirates seized two South Korean fishing boats, held the crews hostage for five months, and immediately demanded a ransom for their release. As negotiations dragged on for months, the pirates beat and starved the crew releasing them only after they received the funds.

In late October 2007, Somali pirates hijacked the *MV Golden Nori*, a 12,000-ton Japanese chemical tanker carrying a load of benzene. This chemical is used in a variety of manufacturing processes and solvents and as an additive to gasoline. If spilled into the environment, serious pollution can result. Exposure to the chemical can cause sudden death. Chronic exposure can result in cancer and Acute Myelogenous Leukemia.

Imagine the potential scenario of a dangerous chemical-laden vessel under the control of pirates. The region lacks international security cooperation for piracy incidents leaving few resources to respond to attacks or a large environmental incident. If a dangerous chemical spill occurred, exclusion areas might take days to establish allowing multiple targets for pirates operating at will in the region. According to the U.S. Navy, there are at least 200 pirates operating in the area.

It seems nothing is sacred with Somali pirates. World Food Program (WFP) ships regularly face attacks. Pirates hijacked the *MV Rozen*, a cargo ship carrying food and aid supplies to their own people. The attack occurred nearly 200 miles from the Somali coast showing the long-range capability of pirates to target and hijack vessels at sea. After 41 days and a ransom paid, the pirates released the crew. During a news interview after the incident, the ships' Captain said the pirates told him they were interested in tankers and container ships because they yield higher ransoms.

When pirates attack, it impacts the global economy. Ships are detained or stolen, crews are injured and sometimes killed and cargoes are lost. With each incident, maritime shipping firms are faced with cargo losses and the payout of high ransoms. Sometimes attacks are not reported attempting to prevent maritime insurers from raising already expensive premiums. In the end, confidence of safe global shipping is in jeopardy. Pirates making millions each year continue to buy weapons and new communications technologies to build upon their organized crime network. As these networks grow, their logistical and internal intelligence capability increases. Over time, there are more loyal to the network than those seeking to prevent attacks. The same methodology continues much like organized drug and alien smuggling operations have for years. Terrorist organizations operate the same way.

In this chapter, we have seen how pirates can attack at will in some regions of the globe. Their attacks are not isolated to losses for the shipping companies alone; the result affects the global economy. This is particularly true in some strategic shipping lanes.

Because of few coalition partners fighting the piracy problem, we've seen that an environmental catastrophe in isolated areas increases the potential hunting ground for pirates. We know that terror groups model operations after successful crime networks. Many of the issues and lessons learned by pirates could easily be put into action by a terror group.

Chapter Eleven

Liquefied Natural Gas (LNG) Vessels

For many, the perception of a Liquefied Natural Gas (LNG) ship is likened to that of a floating bomb waiting to explode. Rather than publish accurate facts it is sometimes easier for the media to portray a scenario leaving behind devastated cities, mass casualties and an environmental catastrophe.

While many reports are published through innocent error, there are some exploiting this dreadful depiction in an attempt to pursue agendas or sell books and videos. After all, gas burns and gas explodes. Given that focus, it is easy to believe that a large ship carrying gas will wreak havoc to a populated area through a massive explosion. I admit that I believed the same until poring through the research to see what professionals working in the industry have to say.

Even so, whenever the discussion of LNG storage and shipping arises, environmentalists will generally recount the devastation from an incident in Ohio. The motivation behind the retelling of this story is not to recount truthful events, but rather, pursue a specific agenda. In order to provide a balanced discussion, the episode in Ohio is noted below.

In 1944, an accident occurred at an LNG storage facility in Cleveland, Ohio. Known as a "Peak-Shaving" facility, surplus natural gas was stored to meet the peak demand during summer and winter periods. At the time, the U.S. was in the midst of World War II and stainless steel alloys were difficult to obtain for construction of a new tank.

Shortly after being placed into service, the tank fractured and LNG spilled into the local sewer system. As the super-cooled gas began to return to atmospheric temperature, a vapor cloud formed within the sewer and later ignited. In the end, there were 128 deaths from this unfortunate accident. The follow-on investigation revealed the inner tank was constructed of 3.5 percent nickel which, when exposed to the sub-freezing temperature of LNG becomes brittle and susceptible to fractures.

The Cleveland incident is the result of faulty materials and structural failure – not an inherent failure of LNG. Another possible causal factor to the accident was the location of the facility. The peak-shaving facility was situated near both a railroad yard and a manufacturing plant used to stamp bombshells in support of the war effort. The combination of the constant vibration and a poorly constructed tank might have been a cause of the quickened structural failure, causing the spill.

This is not to suggest that no dangers associated with LNG vessels exist – there are. Yet, it is vital that an informed decision based upon facts is made, rather than rely upon unknowing fears. There are important issues for first responders involved with a potential LNG-related incident; those will be noted ahead. For now, it is important to debunk the myths and share the facts about LNG ships. The truth will prepare first responders to implement the correct actions of a critical incident management system.

The Facts

Liquefied Natural Gas has been safely transported around the globe since 1959 when the first LNG vessel, a converted World War II freighter made the first transatlantic LNG voyage from Louisiana to the United Kingdom. As LNG is pumped into the cargo tanks, it is frozen to a temperature of -260 degrees Fahrenheit. At that temperature, LNG is neither explosive nor flammable.

If an LNG tank ruptures due to collision, grounding or other incident, the liquefied gas pools on the surface of the water. As the gas begins to warm, it vaporizes and dissipates into the atmosphere. This is a point where an LNG spill can become dangerous to populated areas. If the vapors enter populated areas, there is a potentially dangerous asphyxiation hazard to citizens. Additionally, boat crews and first responders are susceptible if vapors drift into confined spaces.

Another hazard with an LNG spill is the potential for ignition of either the LNG pools or vapor clouds. Even so, the gas-to-air mixture must be within the combustible range of 5.3 to 14.0 percent, and there needs to be an ignition source. When below the lower limit, there is too little fuel for ignition and when above the upper limit, there is too little oxygen.

There are two types of LNG fires: vapor cloud fires and pool fires. The pool fire is the result of the liquid spill floating atop the water. If conditions are within the combustible range and there is an ignition source, a pool fire can ignite. On the other hand, a vapor cloud fire results from the LNG returning to a vapor state as the frozen liquid heats. As wind drives the vapor cloud into confined spaces or over populated areas the cloud can ignite if within the combustible range and ignition source exists. Vapor cloud fires are generally short-lived as the fuel source quickly burns off.

Even so, the likelihood of secondary fires can occur if the vapor cloud burns near other combustible materials. If there is an LNG fire, the most likely impact to a populated area is the heat. LNG burns much hotter than other petroleum fires because it burns cleaner and without smoke. In a typical oil fire, the smoke absorbs some of the heat. The potential for heat hazard, asphyxiation or confined gases will greatly depend upon environmental factors such as the wind, waves, precipitation and humidity.

To get a true understanding of the heat generated by an LNG fire, surface emissive temperature is measured by kilowatts of heat per square meter (kW/m^2). With a heat index value of 5 kW/m^2, a person will receive second-degree burns if exposed for 30-seconds. Steel structures begin to fail with a heat index value of 37.5 kW/m^2. What does this mean? An estimated 30-second exposure to an LNG fire can cause burns up to 2000 meters away and the heat will exceed 200 kW/m^2.

In 2004, Sandia National Laboratories studied the effects of a 5 square meter hole in a tank with a spill size of 12,500 cubic meters of LNG. The surface emissive heat of the fire ranged between 220 to 350 kW/m^2. That is far beyond the amount of heat needed to damage steel structures. The overall duration of the fire lasted for 8 minutes with a heat hazard range of approximately 1,600 meters. It's important to note at this point that the estimated surface emissive heat during the 2001 World Trade Center attack was somewhere between 200 to 250 kW/m^2.

The American Bureau of Shipping (ABS) studied the effect of a hole less than 1 square meter with the same 12,500 cubic meter quantity. The ABS study increased the duration of the fire to 51 minutes with a heat hazard of 265 kW/m^2 and a 650-meter distance. In the case of a smaller hole used in the ABS scenario, there is a likelihood of increased structural damage to the vessel and adjoining tanks. The reasoning for this is because of a slower spill capability. With a smaller hole, the LNG spills out of the vessel slower, hampering the ability to evaporate into the atmosphere, increasing the fire duration and surface emissive heat.

Ships that transport LNG are configured with multiple tanks. Given the heat hazard of a fire resulting from an LNG spill, what are the chances of a cascading failure of adjacent tanks? To answer that question we need to go back and look at the Sandia Labs study of 2004. In a five-tank configuration, Sandia determined that three of the five tanks would be involved if there were a prolonged fire.

An inherent danger of a multi-tank spill is that the flow of LNG is released faster, thereby creating pools that spread over larger areas. If ignition occurs, the heat hazard could extend out to over 2,100 meters. This extended heat area increases the potential for secondary fires and in effect, pushes back first responders attempting to control the scene.

The Response

Given the facts noted above, if there is a marine casualty of an LNG vessel due to grounding, collision or terrorist attack, what response measures can be taken? Because LNG dissipates into the atmosphere, there is little, if any environmental damage from a spill or fire, other than aquatic life affected by pool fires or resulting pollution caused by the incident.

Another important point is that an LNG spill does not always guarantee there will be a resulting fire. The goal is to prevent a fire by containing the spilled LNG in a safe area and preventing ignition sources. Yet, if an LNG fire occurs resulting from a terrorist attack, the likely source of ignition will be an incendiary weapon. This is no secret. Terrorists prefer things that go bang. Explosives always have a psychological impact, cause readily apparent damage and make for good news stories. Given the weapon scenario, the potential for a fire exists, but is short-lived and will last only for the duration it takes for the LNG to burn off. If there is no fire, then the risks are asphyxiation and freeze burns while attempting to contain it.

Typically, fuel fires are extinguished with a foam/water mix. The water helps cool the heat source while the foam lays down a blanket atop the fire in a smothering action. If large quantities of foam are available and there is a delivery means (fireboats, other vessels with pumps, fire hoses, etc.) this might be a recommended approach. However, because of the heat hazard distance, this option may not be available.

If pools can be pushed near abandoned areas of shoreline then perhaps the fire can be attacked from both fireboats and the shore at the same time with foam. This approach is purely speculative and the challenge may be getting near the fire because of the heat. Each locale has unique geographical challenges for fighting such a fire and each incident may react differently to environmental conditions.

When attempting to contain an LNG fire from the water, first responders should never place themselves between the pool and the ship. If the ship fire is not contained and an LNG fire re-flashes, the ignition will rapidly burn toward the source placing first responders in a dangerous spot.

Immediately after an incident, the source of the spill of fire must be contained and rendered safe. Ideally, the vessel should have emergency procedures in place onboard the ship to stop forward motion and drop anchor. If a fire gets out of control or the crew becomes disabled from asphyxiation or other injury, a drifting vessel heading toward a bridge, port facility or grounding ashore risks additional tank failures and in effect, moves the heat or vapor hazard closer to populated areas.

Once the vessel is stationary, there is a greater capability of containing the spill. Coast Guard Marine Inspectors, Investigators and Environmental Response personnel will likely pursue this option. In all likelihood, a temporary repair of the tank may not be possible because of oxygen depleting vapors and the high risk of freeze burns from the super-cooled LNG. Once the LNG spills to a level below the hole, safe transfer of the remaining cargo might be an option after the entire area is under control.

First responders, including boat coxswains should be equipped with full-face protection and air breathing equipment. They should also have thermal protective gear. The three greatest threats to first responders are freeze burns from spills, asphyxiation from gases and heat from resulting fires.

In an event of this nature, air and surface exclusion areas must be maintained. While the surface emissive power of the fire will generally keep unwanted boats out of the area, an incident like this will generally draw good Samaritans wanting to help. These boats, if not fully equipped with pumps and breathing apparatus can risk asphyxiated crews drifting into the pool fires exacerbating the situation.

The air exclusion area is critical. As the heated LNG returns to a vapor state, a cloud of potentially combustible gas will begin to rise into the atmosphere. Engine heat from news helicopters wanting the best shot could in effect ignite a vapor cloud fire, placing all first responders in jeopardy.

News helicopters became a real burden during search and recovery of the TWA-800 incident. During that incident, my job was to monitor and enforce the initial air and sea exclusion areas and define the search blocks used during the operation. As the air controller for Coast Guard aircraft, one pilot called back and told me he had just experienced a near miss by a network news helicopter getting in their way. I had to get a call patched through to the news agency and have a senior person divert them from the area.

In an attempt to get the latest-breaking story, news helicopters will sometimes cross exclusion areas and disregard safety of flight issues. An unfortunate example of focusing on the story and not situational awareness occurred during a July 2007 Phoenix, Arizona police chase when two news helicopters collided and crashed, killing four. It is vital that air and surface exclusion areas be included, acknowledged, and understood by the press in critical response plans of LNG incidents. An aircraft incident over an LNG spill could amplify the incident by placing first responders in greater jeopardy.

Terrorist Benefits of an LNG Attack

The resulting impact of an LNG attack by terrorists stirs fear. Many people understand there is an inherent danger with LNG vessels. They just don't know why. It is easy for a person to assume that large tanks full of natural gas are under pressure similar to a large propane tank. At the very least, the uninformed will believe that LNG tanks will explode. After all, houses heated with natural gas explode every year; why wouldn't a ship? We now know from reading the facts earlier that this is not the case. The public engaged in day-to-day living does not know that.

This uncertainty and fear causes citizens to question their safety and the ability of our government to protect them. This is precisely the place where a terrorist wants us – unsure. The terrorist then benefits by prime time news coverage augmented by those "Professional Blamers" calling for an investigation.

Secondly, shipments of LNG and other hazardous cargoes will likely cease until the implementation of an increased safety and security posture. After the events of 9/11, all air traffic ceased until the enactment of additional personnel resources and security procedures. Many of these personnel were reserve military also serving within law enforcement, first responders or serving in other local, state or federal government capacities.

While personnel were put in place to secure and augment the needs of the nation, there was the huge economic cost of activating, housing and paying the additional forces. While many of these personnel were serving their local communities, activating and transferring them from small towns around the country short of law enforcement and first responders. In short, augmenting critical areas sometimes opened holes in others.

This is not meant as a criticism as frankly, I don't know what else could have been done. As a nation, we pulled together and as a nation, we needed to show the world that we are back in business and taking action. Given that, the reserve call-up was the right thing to do. Nonetheless, the point is response to a terrorist attack becomes a huge resource drain. Looking back at the 9/11 attacks and the resulting years afterward as a guide, critical incident management plans should incorporate such resource losses as part of future incident planning.

A third way a terrorist would benefit from an LNG attack (or any substantive attack for that matter) would be the economic impact. There is a certain expectation of a stock market drop due to uncertain conditions. When the impact is significant, both Asian and European markets will mirror the initial uncertainty. Even so, after awhile, the market will stabilize as it historically does. In an LNG incident however, the costs of heating fuel in the northeast will rise, maritime insurers may increase premiums or hesitate to insure those vessels considered as targets. The result will influence shippers and the supporting industries worldwide and increase the cost of imported goods to the U.S.

A Review

Throughout this chapter, we have looked at the perceptions of the LNG industry, some verifiable facts and possible response issues for those personnel tasked with responding to an incident. We now know that ships with super-cooled LNG will not explode and the fuel will not burn unless certain conditions exist. When it comes to an issue like LNG, first responders must be accurately informed of the hazards and know there are possible options at their disposal. This is how we keep our people safe. Anything less is like sending someone into hell with a fire extinguisher.

Chapter Twelve

High Occupancy Vessels and the Terrorist Threat

Terrorists clearly want to kill Americans and citizens from Western cultures. The 1998 Usama bin Laden fatwa reiterates the point that Islamic terror groups should take every opportunity to strike. It is likely that high volume passenger vessels are on the radar of those intending to target innocent civilians.

The larger passenger vessels are targets in waiting for a terrorist attack. In many places around the globe, these large passenger ships function on tight operating schedules and generally have a minimum complement of security personnel. Once a vessel departs the pier, there is no guarantee of safe passage.

In recent years, cruise ships and ferry systems have come to the forefront as potential terrorist targets. While these vessels can be likely targets, the threat doesn't stop there. In fact, some vessel operators make it easier for a terrorist group to target them.

Large casino vessels operate along the rivers in isolated areas. Yet, one in particular, a multilevel vessel modeled after an 1800's styled paddle wheeler, advertises on the Internet how they carry 3,000 passengers. Many cities and tourist areas with a waterside view offer dinner cruises. One boat operator advertises online the ability to carry up to 450 passengers at one time.

Many years ago, I often sailed onboard a large entertainment vessel operating along the Mississippi River in New Orleans. Each night, the ship would carry nearly two thousand passengers for a three-hour trip along the river and back. During the transit, various music concerts would keep the passengers engaged and the onboard bars would keep them drunk.

If there had been a terror attack, it is likely that passengers unfamiliar with the layout of the vessel would quickly become disoriented exacerbating any chance of a safe egress. The same vessel is now located along another portion of the river with a different purpose. Even so, when there are large numbers of passengers onboard vessels that transit away from a ready response, these vessels make for an easy prey by the terrorist.

Unlike an incident occurring on land, a terrorist attack onboard a floating vessel adds an extra challenge to those responding to the incident. A ship is constantly on the move. If the vessels' engineering or steering systems are damaged, the ship becomes an uncontrollable hulk, driven by the currents. If an attack occurs along a narrow navigational channel, then there is the possibility of grounding or an allision with bridge structures.

A fire onboard the vessel may rage out of control because the prevailing wind around the vessel feeds the flames. There are further risks associated with fuel and oil fires from onboard storage tanks. A shipboard fire easily becomes a large confined space, filled with potentially toxic gases from burning and smoldering materials.

Response issues can become extremely challenging for responders attempting to get to a floating vessel in distress. Many responders are unfamiliar with the layout of many of the larger boats operating in their area and specific issues effectively fighting a fire at sea. In many cases, fire personnel attempt to maintain a standoff distance and cool the vessel so they can later get onboard. Finally, there is the possibility of the vessel sinking out from under them.

In an earlier chapter, I discussed training issues for first responders and the importance of regularly conducting realistic exercises. First responders need to be fully aware of the types of vessels operating in their areas, the hazards associated with each vessel and understand the numbers of passengers they may face during a crisis.

Training should be similar to that conducted by personnel serving on our larger naval ships and Coast Guard Cutters. In that environment, the crews are required to know the entire vessel, where the dangerous areas are and how to get out. A tabletop exercise will do nothing but kill first responders. Rescue personnel should ride and become familiar with the vessels; their lives and the lives of those they may have to save might depend on it.

So far, in this chapter, I have identified the possibility of attacks against large volumes of isolated passengers and some challenges of rescuing them. I'm not providing information that a terror group doesn't already know about. In an earlier chapter, I said that a terrorist group doesn't need my help finding vulnerable areas. In fact, the terrorist can get plenty of ideas, thanks to the Hollywood movie industry.

A recent Hollywood movie depicted a terror attack on a large passenger and auto ferry. Shortly after it left the dock in New Orleans, the ferry exploded from a vehicle-borne Improvised Explosive Device (VBIED). While much of the movie was unrealistic and designed for sensationalist entertainment, I began to think how likely an attack like this is.

Our ferry systems carry hundreds of vehicles across waterways each day. In this scenario, the attack occurred on a river with a high current. Depending on the location of a VBIED detonation, the vessel could be rendered inoperable and much of the evidence washed downriver. Is this an unlikely scenario? Absolutely not. Terrorist and insurgent elements throughout the world use this tactic on a regular basis. As a nation, we have seen VBIED attacks against our own nation during the first World Trade Center attack and in Oklahoma City with the attack on the Murrah Building.

The owners of large passenger vessels operate as a moneymaking business. Given that, many clearly advertise the vessel arrangement, the potential capacity of passengers, provide maps of their transit routes and their sailing schedules. This is not a bad thing...this is business. Operators want potential passengers to see what they offer and what they may see along the route.

We live in an information-centric society. Knowledge is power and the ready access to information systems allows us greater opportunities to live freely, learn and gain an understanding of things to make life better. Yet, these same constructive information tools allow terrorists a targeting opportunity against us. It is vital to incorporate this concept into emergency management planning.

Each agency expected to participate in an incident response operation should investigate potential capabilities and knowledge an adversary can gain from their desktop computer. What live video camera feeds provide online surveillance and targeting? What does an online advertisement tell adversaries that are hoping to target vessels and kill the innocent?

Ferry Systems

A well-known west coast ferry operator states on their website the ability to carry between 325 and 725 passengers in a single transit. Another ferry service operating between the U.S. and British Columbia describes a capability of carrying 2,500 passengers and over 60 vehicles.

On February 27, 2004, the 510-foot *Superferry 14* was sailing near Corregidor Island in the Philippines with 877 passengers. At 11:00 PM, a man walked onboard the ferry with a television set in a cardboard box. Packed within the box was nearly 8 pounds (3.6 kg) of explosives. An hour later, the bomb exploded.

The detonation ignited a fire that burned for over 12-hours. The inferno burned so hot that rescue and recovery crews had to wait for the steel hulk to cool for two days before they could even get onboard. Abu Sayyaf, a local terrorist group took responsibility for the blast.

Because of the complexity of conducting a thorough maritime casualty investigation, it took weeks to know for sure if the incident was the result of terrorists, or the result of a maritime casualty from an engineering failure. In the end, investigators agreed the incident was due to a terrorist attack; 116 were killed and 92 are missing.

Yet, the attacks by Abu Sayyaf didn't stop there. Another ferry, the *M/V Dona Ramona* became victim to a bombing 18-months later. The Philippine passenger ferry was conducting a normal 30-minute transit when an IED exploded near liquefied propane gas (LPG) tanks at the rear of the vessel. The blast injured 30 passengers, including nine children. Three passengers died from injuries by the blast and burns.

In December 1999, an Algerian named Ahmed Ressam boarded the *M/V Coho*, an auto-passenger ferry in Victoria, BC intending to enter the U.S. at the Port Angeles Ferry dock in Washington State. When U.S. Customs inspectors questioned Ressam and asked for additional identification, he panicked and ran from his vehicle. Stashed within the wheel well were jars of nitroglycerin and timing devices for an intended attack at the Los Angeles Airport.

A year earlier, Ressam received training at the Khalden training camp in Afghanistan. Numerous detainees claim that Khalden was not a terrorist camp, but was only for military training. Yet, at least four individuals associated with the first World Trade Center bombing, Richard Reid, the shoe bomber and possibly as many as three of the 9/11 hijackers received training at Khalden. The ferry system was seen as an easy entry point to the U.S. for terrorists. If Ressam kept his wits about him, LAX Airport might have seen a New Years bombing.

In recent years, there have been numerous accounts of Middle-Eastern men thought to be conducting surveillance onboard ferry systems. One account in particular, gives credence to those concerns.

In Seattle, Washington, there were reports of two suspicious Middle-Eastern men on the local ferry system. While these two remain unidentified, law enforcement believes they were conducting surveillance for a possible terror attack. One crewmember photographed them and passed the information to authorities. The pictures of the two individuals were later published in the news. Suddenly the arguments begin. Should these pictures have been published or not?

I tend to think it was a good choice. If they were engaged in pre-operational surveillance, they will likely have a difficult time staying out of sight unless they are part of a larger cell. If they attempt to flee the country, there is a better chance of identifying these guys. At the very least, perhaps an attack was stalled. Note what I said...stalled. Al-Qaeda has a history of retrying unsuccessful attacks. If attacking a soft target like a ferry packed with American citizens is on their targeting radar, then it will eventually happen.

If these two are not associated with a terrorist plot, all they need to do is to come forward and explain why they were pacing the decks and giving the appearance of measuring spaces. Perhaps they can explain why they were in restricted areas on the ferry and taking pictures and studying emergency evacuation rosters. History has shown that photographic surveillance materials are commonly found within safe houses of terror suspects during raids.

Since the story hit the news, some are now claiming these two are being racially profiled. Yet, neither of these two came forward to claim they are innocent victims of racial profiling or explain why they were there. Is this a case where silence validates the concerns?

We are living in a country where there are those that want to kill us. Even so, we have organizations operating within our country seeking to squelch our ability to report issues of concern. I tend to think that some of these, "Special interest" groups exist because there is big business in complainers. If the group listens to them with concerned looks on their faces, they'll get donations.

Maybe I'm a critic; maybe I'm a realist. It seems that if a report is submitted and the individual is identified as Middle Eastern, it is racial profiling. No, it is not. Monitoring the environment around us for security threats is common sense in today's world. If we remain alert for someone that behaves suspiciously, it is behavioral profiling and race or culture should not play a role.

Yet, ironically, this is exactly where our adversary wants us to be - in a place where we are afraid to report their activities. After all, call it profiling and then the reporter becomes the villain.

So there is no doubt about where I am going, let me just say this: racial or cultural profiling is bad; behavioral profiling is a good thing. Criminals and idiots come from all over the world. If we aware of activities that could hurt us, and we report it, that is a good thing.

Federal investigators looking into the 9/11 attack believe that two of the hijackers entered the U.S. via a ferry transiting from Nova Scotia to Maine. Given this history of criminal activity onboard ferry systems, it is naïve to suggest that this mode of the Maritime Transportation System will not be targeted. Public records from the Bureau of Transportation Statistics show that in 2006, there were 691 ferries operating within U.S. navigable waters.

Cruise Ships

In October 1985, four members from the Palestinian Liberation Front (PLF) took the crew of the Italian Cruise ship *Achille Lauro* hostage. They demanded the immediate release of 50 PLF members imprisoned for terrorist activities in Israel. If their demands were not met, the terrorists would begin killing American passengers.

During the ordeal, the terrorist shot and killed Leon Klinghoffer, a 69-year old handicapped American. He was killed because he was Jewish. Mr. Klinghoffer and his wife Marilyn were celebrating their 36th wedding anniversary. Afterward, his body was thrown into the sea with his wheelchair.

While the terrorists sought freedom for their cohorts in prison, I will reiterate an earlier point made in this book. To include terrorist activity with freedom fighting is to elevate the position of cowards.

Killing an innocent man in a wheelchair is an act of cowardice.

After two days, the hijackers surrendered in exchange for a pledge of safe passage. While this appears to be a failed attempt in an effort to free fellow terrorists, this operation yielded three benefits: the heightened media exposure, a new level of credibility measured by the Special Forces response, and the emotional horror of a defenseless victim – no one is safe, not even the handicapped.

This incident was not unlike a senseless killing in June of the same year. During a hijacking of a TWA plane, U.S. Navy diver Robert Stethem was killed and his body thrown to the tarmac. Intentional kidnapping and hostage taking by terrorist groups are intended to become a media event. The terrorist views this form of action as a win-win strategy. They make demands of governments and barter for the lives of their captives. If the demands are met, they gain credibility to their cause. Yet, even if the demands are not met, they gain media exposure.

In the case of the *Achille Lauro* incident, terrorists used the maritime nexus as a vehicle to shock the world by the heinous murder of a handicapped American, raising the bar of terrorism one notch higher.

Near the end of 2002, passengers from three separate cruise ships began experiencing gastrointestinal viruses. Each instance occurred near the same time. Different cruise lines departing from different ports operate each of these ships. One of the ships was struck several times. In all, over 1,000 passengers became ill. According to a report from the Miami Herald, *"CDC officials have said there is no evidence that the cruise ship outbreaks are the work of terrorists".*

Although, after an exhaustive investigation, the CDC has been unable to definitively state the outbreak was *not* a preliminary trial run for a more deadly WMD incident. To be fair to the cruise industry it should be noted that the New York Times stated the cause of this outbreak was the result of person-to-person contact. Still, it is coincidental that each of these cases occurred concurrently.

In the world of bio-terrorism, it takes only a small amount of a toxin like anthrax, botulism, brucellosis or tularemia to infect a large group of people. In 1984, the Rajneesh Foundation infected salad bars in different restaurants with salmonella. Their intent was to sway a local election by making people too sick to vote. Hundreds fell ill from the attack. This scenario is an easy replay onboard cruise ships with large volumes of contained people and easy access to an unending food line.

During a recent cruise, I observed a few issues related to both safety and security. Because of new Transportation Security Administration (TSA) policy, passengers are separated from their luggage at the airport terminal. This baggage is out of the passengers' control for 2-3 hours.

During the check-in process, the attendant asked for a passport or other identification. I presented a completed immigration form and a U.S. passport. The screening attendant never opened my passport, looked at the picture or name, nor did he ever check for a valid identification. With that, I was issued my boarding pass/stateroom access key.

While the check-in procedure does become a long and tedious process, particularly when screening over 1,300 passengers, a simple review of human factors would suggest there is the potential to make mistakes. Cruise ship operators should pursue the use of biometric identification systems to aide the check-in process.

With the increased use of fraudulent identification, passports and visas, access becomes far too easy. Some of the hijackers from the 9/11 attack utilized passports with fraudulent stamps or other indicators of terrorist activities. Granted, some passengers will complain; but that is the price of security.

Casino Boats

As I noted earlier in this chapter, casino boats are another type of high occupancy vessel that often carries over 3,000 people. While these vessels normally have a strong security force, their purpose is to detect cheaters and protect the money, not necessarily the passengers during a terror attack. Nor are they trained in counter terrorist operations. To an Islamic terror group, a casino could represent all that is contrary to their beliefs. While casinos hold large numbers of people, they also give representation of the capitalistic society they fight against. The typical gambler remains focused upon the table or the slot machine. This environment becomes easy to place an explosive device, as few would see it coming.

In April 1998, a towboat pushing 14 barges lost control and struck a bridge. After the impact, one of the barges broke loose and rammed a large casino boat carrying 2,300 people. Fortunately, no injuries occurred. However, un-inspected vessels like the towboat operate in close proximity of casino boats, ferries and other passenger vessels everyday.

Unlike bombs and guns, a collision with a large vessel is a low-tech option to attack innocent citizens. A maritime casualty to a boat carrying large numbers of people unfamiliar with escape routes leads to panic, panic leads to fatalities, fatalities makes news. News gives terrorists credibility.

A successful maritime attack by a terrorist group would increase the perception of their capabilities and potentially validate their cause. Additionally, each attack shows terror groups around the world the maritime transportation system is vulnerable and ready for another attack.

Chapter Thirteen

The Fishing Vessel Threat

In the earlier chapter dealing with towing vessels, I noted that these vessels are free from inspection unless operated on an international route. Fishing vessels likewise are not held to vessel inspections and have few regulatory obligations. Larger commercial and passenger vessels are regulated according to 46 Code of Federal Regulations (Shipping).

These regulations clarify the standard of safe operation, dictate structural integrity, and fire fighting and lifesaving concerns. Given that, fishing boats are similar to towing vessels because there is absolutely no confidence of the mechanical or structural condition.

Even so, fishing industry representatives have successfully lobbied against regulation claiming they operate on small profit margins and can't afford to bring vessels up to the standard required for a Certificate of Inspection (COI). After a series of fishing vessel casualties, Congress did finally enact the Commercial Fishing Industry Vessel Safety Act of 1988 in order to mandate the requirement for safety and survival equipment. However, aside from regulations pertaining to lifesaving issues, vessel inspection requirements are noticeably absent. While the Coast Guard offers voluntary safety inspections, those reputable operators take advantage of this opportunity. Yet, few mandated regulations exist.

Previously we looked at the ability of small fishing vessels to impede the safe navigation of larger commercial vessels and gave an example of a near-tragedy by the Oakland Bay Bridge caused by a fisherman. Because of the lack of oversight toward fishing boats, there is a much greater chance of reckless operation as the bridge incident shows.

Looking back at the chapter dealing with the sailors, there is a proficiency expectation for merchant mariners operating the larger commercial ships and charter vessels. These mariners are required to undergo numerous training courses, pass written and physical tests as well as be subject to random drug testing. Then, there is the moral standard: They undergo criminal background checks and cannot serve if they have drug or alcohol dependencies. Fishing vessel operators are another story. They *may* take an examination for a license; however, there is no requirement. There are no proficiency prerequisites, no criminal background checks and no drug testing. If an individual can buy the boat, they can sail it without regulation other than an infrequent safety or fisheries boarding by the Coast Guard.

Drug Manufacture and Trafficking

When I was supporting the Office of Law Enforcement with the Coast Guard, we began observing the potential for drug manufacture and trafficking within the commercial fishing fleets. Discussions with other law enforcement personnel around the country indicate that fishing boats have operators or crews with criminal records or association to Outlaw Motorcycle Gangs (OMG).

Precursor Chemicals used Onboard Fishing Vessels

Refrigeration systems onboard fishing boats generally use anhydrous ammonia or freon to keep the fish cold. Both chemicals are precursors for methamphetamine manufacture. Another precursor chemical sometimes used on these vessels is ether, used as a starting fluid for engines. All of these chemicals present serious hazards to first responders. Of particular concern is anhydrous. Inhalation of this chemical brings about severe respiratory injuries or death at higher concentrations. As a corrosive, it can burn the skin or eyes.

Anhydrous is often concealed within fire extinguishers and portable propane cylinders. When stored within unsuitable pressure containers, anhydrous corrodes the brass fittings from the inside out, leaving a telltale sign of a blue-green residue on the valve stem. This corrosion in turn weakens the integrity of the pressurized cylinder. A brass fitting appearing to be intact may break off causing a hazardous chemical release as well as the uncontrolled flight of the container.

Drug History onboard Fishing Vessels

In 2003, an Indiana man suffered severe injuries when a fire extinguisher carrying anhydrous exploded, burning his body and causing serious lung damage. In August 2003, law enforcement arrested three crewmen from the fishing vessel, "*NU-C*" in Westport, WA after authorities discovered a methamphetamine lab aboard the boat.

In Lighthouse Point, FL, Law Enforcement discovered 771 pounds of cocaine hidden in the forward cabin area of the vessel, "*Sea Double*". In June 2000, investigators arrested two individuals from Northern California who had faked their deaths 11 years earlier by sinking their fishing boat. These two individuals according to U.S. Customs and DEA were responsible for the import of over 400 tons of hashish and marijuana through their fleet of fishing vessels.

Many smugglers use fishing boats as drug transport vessels. Smugglers import their load into the country by blending in with existing fishing fleets as they make entry to the U.S. While there are many reputable fishermen working the waters, the potential for drug manufacture or trafficking continues as these vessels and operators are not held to regulation. Additionally, small privately owned boats used as live-aboard vessels could shield clandestine operations.

Indicators of Suspicious Activities

So far, in this chapter we've looked at the potential for criminal activities onboard fishing vessels. Recall that I said in an earlier chapter that terrorist groups often operate through many of the same criminal enterprises found in organized crime. Given that, let's look at some indicators of fishing vessels that might point to suspicious activities related to terrorism, surveillance activities, bomb making or drug manufacture.

- A fishing vessel departs port and returns showing no indication of fishing activity. An indicator would include dry fishing gear, the wrong gear for the type of intended catch, or sometimes, no catch at all.

- A fishing vessel returning to port may have, "Rub marks" along the hull indicating they may have rendezvoused with another vessel for an onload or offload of cargo.

- Live aboard vessels may have frequent visitors, staying for short durations. If they are anchored away from the mooring area, they may intend to avoid direct observation by law enforcement. Are the windows darkened or show evidence of electronic surveillance equipment? A Passive Infrared (PIR) motion sensor or video surveillance camera offers the occupants early warning. Are the vessels located in an area where operators could conduct surveillance activities of passing cargo ships, passenger vessels or port facilities?

- A fishing vessel secretes a strong chemical or urine smell indicative of ammonia, acetone or other substance. Do the occupants bring mason jars, large amounts of camp stove fuel or pressure cylinders onboard the vessel? This could indicate a drug or bomb manufacturing operation. Do the occupants frequently go outside to smoke, or not smoke on the vessel at all? It might be worth looking into.

- What indicators of drug or bomb making materials are found in the dumpsters at the pier? Is there evidence of precursor chemicals, coffee filters and sometimes diapers to filter chemicals? Duct tape, various containers, hoses and kitty litter are indicators of a chemical operation common with methamphetamine manufacture. Do they take their trash away from the nearby dumpster?

Terror Incidents and Fishing Vessels

The October 2002 attack against the French tank ship *MV Limburg* was the result of a small fiberglass resin fishing boat used as a suicide boat. The attack occurred 12 miles from shore, a distance easily manageable for a fishing boat, yet near enough for quick news coverage to broadcast the event.

In November 2000, members of the Hamas terrorist group attempted a suicide operation using a fishing boat to attack Israeli forces patrolling the coastline. In January 2006, the Tamil Tigers attacked a Sri Lankan patrol vessel with a fishing boat loaded with explosives. The attack killed 13 Sri Lankan sailors. In May 2003, an Egyptian fishing boat, the *Abu Hassan* attempted a smuggling operation by bringing weapons, missiles and bomb making materials and instructions into the Gaza Strip. Israeli naval patrols spotted and captured the vessel before it could reach port.

Each year, individuals buy fishing vessels with no proven ability to operate them safely. The vessels are under minimal regulatory oversight and the veracity of the operator may be questionable. Transnational criminal groups learned a long time ago that fishing boats are a unique transportation mechanism because they are outside the scope of enforcement. In effect, out of sight, out of mind.

We have discussed how these vessels have a history of supporting the drug trade and weapons smuggling. We should not overlook the possibility that they can smuggle high interest aliens into the country, serve as a surveillance platform, or, as seen above, participate in direct attack operations.

Chapter Fourteen

Cargo Theft and Containerships

Throughout this text, I discussed the importance of the maritime nexus as being a critical element of international commerce. Given that, the freight conduit of the Maritime Transportation System incorporates truck, sea and rail systems to move shipments. Because of the large volume of freight leaving ships for follow-on transfer to alternate transportation mechanisms, cargo theft has become a very big business.

The International Cargo Security Council (ICSC) estimates that cargo theft places the loss at $25 billion per year. The U.S. Maritime Administration statistics in 2006 reports that there were 19,591 calls to U.S. ports by containerships larger than 10,000 deadweight tons of carrying capacity. A typical container ship may carry between 2,000 to 3,000 containers in a single load. According to Hapag-Lloyd, one of their ships, the *Hamburg Express*, is capable of carrying, 8,750 containers.

Preventing cargo theft is generally not on the radar screen of local law enforcement. It is not that law enforcement doesn't care; they simply lack the appropriate resources. This is even more so since 9/11. Law enforcement personnel were reassigned to other homeland security related missions and continue an emphasis for enforcement actions against local crime. For years, the exact cargo theft figures within the U.S. were unknown and unreported. If declared, it is bad for business and increases insurance premiums for the shipper.

Fortunately, the ICSC proactively sought accountability measures and helped include cargo theft into the renewed version of the PATRIOT Act of March 9, 2006. The value to this initiative now requires an accounting of the problem and inclusion into the Uniform Crime Reporting (UCR) System. By tying the issue to the PATRIOT Act, stiffer penalties apply for a conviction. It is important to note that including enforcement under the PATRIOT Act is not a ploy to obtain convictions. The current scale of cargo theft is a serious threat to our national economic state. Incorporating this important crime metric into the UCR helps apply funding and proper law enforcement resources. In turn, stronger enforcement may prevent tampering with the many containers rolling through our cities each day. As you'll see in the pages ahead, this issue, from a terrorism perspective is not an attractive one at all.

Years ago, as a maritime investigator I was conducting crew interviews of a containership that had a recent marine casualty. The ship was moored at a large west coast container transfer facility. While departing the yard, I drove through a large maze of containers. It was very easy to get disoriented in the midst of this large labyrinth of steel boxes stacked atop one another. I noticed that while I was driving around this huge yard attempting to find my way out, I didn't see any security personnel. At one point, being curious about the container security, I stopped to examine some of the containers. No one ever challenged me. Access control to the staged containers was non-existent.

Asset protection is an important issue. The specifics of the cargo should be protected in order to deny opportunities for theft. Yet, the entire shipping process requires a variety of personnel. As an example, the system begins with those tasked with the initial shipping, then the truck drivers, dock or railroad workers and those working within the container yards. As we saw in the chapter dealing with piracy, there were some cases when robbers knew to open specific cargo containers, indicating the possibility that they have had access to the vessel or were in collusion with others having shipping and cargo information.

According to numerous interviews I've had with anonymous sources in the industry, depending upon the port, it is not uncommon to find cargo bill of lading forms in the trash. This provides the criminal element a virtual shopping list. While new security procedures are in place for entry and exit of trucks at container yards, strict control should be imposed upon where trucks travel, how long they stay there and proper accountability for the cargo they are taking with them.

There are existing technologies allowing for secure staging areas, surveillance and the accountability of the container facilities. Yet, implementation becomes both a funding and a time issue, each affecting the flow of commerce. The current locking mechanisms and small metal seals used are inexpensive. Radio Frequency Identification (RFID) or GPS tracking systems are available on the market for greater security. Yet, these options increase the costs and shippers are reticent to limit profits by using these new devices.

Some ports now claim they have a 100 percent inspection rate of containers. The are a number of x-ray and scanning inspection systems that conduct density checks and search for anomalies indicative of an explosive device. Even so, while some ports do an initial scan of each container leaving the port facility, it is unrealistic given the numbers of containers entering the U.S. to expect that the contents of each one is fully accounted for. Realistically, only a small percentage of the millions of containers transiting through our ports each year are fully scanned.

Then there are instances when the result of a scan forces the opening of a container for a manual inspection. The secondary inspection is a good thing if there were a real threat imposed by an explosive cargo. On the other hand, there is the risk of compromising the integrity of the container contents. The possibility of cargo theft increases.

While some scanners will look for evidence of a nuclear or radiological device, we still have the issue of effectively identifying a chemical or biological cargo unless there is knowledge of the substance or toxin. Each of these scans takes time and is expensive. This economic cost is one of the greatest impediments to effective implementation – one the criminal and terrorist element is clearly aware of and seeks to exploit.

The discussion of cargo containers and terrorism inevitably includes nuclear devices or radiological dirty bombs. Certainly, terrorists want the capability of nuclear or radiological weapons, but frankly, I don't believe that is where our threat will come from in the near term. With the threat of trans-national weapons proliferation, that day may get here. Even then, such a weapon would most likely arrive by way of another type of un-inspected (or rarely inspected) vessel.

It is important to look back at history and study the methodologies used by terrorists. Al-Qaeda for instance, is a group of cost benefit experts. They will use what they can to get the biggest bang without the need of high-technology methods. Their weapons include conventional bombs, small boats and airplanes. Their methodology is to blow things up, crash into them or both. We should look back, review where we have been within this book, and see our potential threats ahead. These are a few likely threat scenarios:

First, as we have seen, small vessels can impede cargo ships and precipitate grounding or cause them to crash into bridges or other infrastructure. If the shipping port closes, the economy suffers and the terrorist succeeds. Looking back at successful small boat attacks by terrorist elements, we see that a *MV Limburg* or *USS Cole* attack might be viable. In the *MV Limburg* incident, the resulting impact of the attack was primarily because of the target choice.

In the case of the *MV Limburg*, the target selection of a tanker exacerbated the situation by the psychological impact of hitting a tank ship, and environmentally with a large oil spill. This scenario, depending on the location of an attack, could shut down a vital waterway and stop maritime commerce to the port. A small boat attack against a large containership *might* offset the stability of the vessel causing some of the above-deck containers to plunge into the waterway. Even so, that may not be a likely scenario unless it was a smaller ship overloaded with containers. Since the inner cargo spaces of the ship are loaded with large quantities of heavy containers, in effect, the internal cargo adds ballast and stability to the vessel.

Second, we have looked at various piracy scenarios that include hijacking. There are some reports of hijackers commandeering a vessel at sea just to practice controlling large ships; and then, after awhile, they depart. Because of the Coast Guard's increased security postures onboard specific vessels, this option becomes tougher for terrorist groups at major ports. Even though, this option is not impossible if a ship outside the current boarding and security criteria is hijacked. Even a smaller cargo vessel with forward motion and tonnage poses a threat against a crowded bridge during commuting hours or, at public waterside areas.

On December 14, 1996, the *M/V Bright Field* crashed into the Riverwalk in New Orleans. The 735-foot cargo ship slammed into the populated tourist area on a Saturday afternoon injuring 66 people. The economic costs exceeded $15 million. While the New Orleans incident resulted from a shipboard mechanical failure, such a large battering ram, when directed against vital infrastructure can be deadly.

A third option is the use of a large conventional explosive device. I described in my earlier chapter, "Understanding Terrorist Methodologies" a hypothetical scenario where sightseers are walking along the pedestrian path of a well-known bridge. As a large cargo ship passes below, the tourists grab their video cameras to capture the unique viewpoint. A pre-placed IED detonates while the tourists capture the moment on video.

Because of the structural integrity of a ship's hull, the odds are against a conventional weapon sinking a vessel. Placement of the bomb, the type and quantity of explosives and a timed detonation offers too many chances for failure. Yet, a highly visible explosion like the one in the hypothetical scenario could hinder the safe navigational control of the vessel and cause it to run aground or strike a bridge.

A fourth possibility is a conventional bomb hidden within the cargo containers. Generally, depending on the size of the explosive device, such a method would have little destructive impact to the vessel unless the container is located deep within the ship. A terrorist using this methodology may not be able to guarantee placement of the container onboard a vessel. Even so, if a container loaded with explosives detonated deep within the ship, other containers surround it and thereby would likely limit the impact of the explosion to the immediate area of the blast. Even if a fire ensued from the explosion, the internal areas of cargo ships have fire protection systems in place. Given that, I believe a conventional weapon attack against the cargo container is unlikely and ineffective.

Lastly, there is the option of a WMD event. While this may be an option in the future, this consideration makes for sensational news and debate at Congressional hearings. We shouldn't live in fear, but we should also consider the most tragic options to build upon our security posture. We live in a world where weapons technology is easily proliferated and terrorism will never be totally eradicated from the globe.

Certainly, a WMD attack via the maritime

transportation system has the capability for tragedy as major ports are near large, heavily populated areas. The worst result would come from a nuclear device and could kill millions. While Al-Qaeda and other adversaries clearly would like that option, they have not shown a capability – yet. If this were a feasible option, there would be indications of explosive testing and that has not happened.

Generally, Al-Qaeda will use technology as part of their planning cycle, but they utilize the low-tech approaches during their attacks. After the 9/11 attacks, U.S. forces attacked the Tarnak Farms training camp in Afghanistan and found that Al-Qaeda experimented with biological warfare (BW) and chemical (CW) agents. To date, they have not carried out any successful attacks using CW or BW agents. If terrorists did conduct a successful BW, CW or dirty-bomb attack, it is unlikely to come from a maritime position unless close to shore and prevailing coastal winds are in their favor. As I said earlier, Al-Qaeda is a group of cost benefit experts. I believe that if an attack of this nature occurred, it would be within populated areas on land.

Given the five options (small boat attack, hijacking, conventional explosives against the ship, the cargo or a WMD event), we need to be prepared for any of the scenarios presented above. The law enforcement and intelligence community should examine each of these scenarios and inject them into their geographic area of operations. How would a terrorist conduct these attacks locally? What are the indicators of a specific attack? What are the worst-case scenarios and what is the likely impact? What is the best way to respond, particularly if response capabilities are lost? These questions need to be addressed today and alternative options considered before an attack comes. There will never be a day when our adversary decides they like us. We are their target.

Last year, I participated in a terrorism course consisting of members throughout law enforcement, the military and the intelligence community. Near the end of the course, various teams collaborated to develop attack methods from the terrorists' perspective. The team I was associated with was mostly law enforcement and we constructed a maritime attack scenario that left everyone in the course wondering how to detect it and how to respond. Because the attack method leaves more questions than answers for responders, I will not describe it in this text to give an adversary an advantage.

Another potential threat that we face within cargo containers is human smuggling. In April 2006, a containership entered the port of Seattle with a hidden cargo of 22 illegal aliens from Shanghai. When working in the San Francisco Bay area, ships arriving at the Port of Oakland regularly had hidden travelers within cargo containers from China. In October 2001, authorities in Gioia Tauro, Italy discovered an Egyptian named Farid Rizk living within a cargo container. He entered the container in Port Said, Egypt intending to travel to Canada.

Stowaways are common within the maritime nexus. When assigned with the Coast Guard in Mobile, AL, I had coverage of a large portion of the Gulf Coast. There were many cases of stowaways coming from various parts of the world onboard freight ships. At certain times of the year, we could almost predict their arrival. Because of weather conditions and the sea state, it was as though there were a "Stowaway Season."

The case of Farid Rizk however, was not a simple stowaway incident. He carried papers claiming he was an aircraft mechanic...in addition to fraudulent credit cards, security passes for various airports, two cell phones, a camera and a laptop computer. Stowaways usually carry nothing more than themselves and maybe a small bag of clothes and some cash. This incident opened the eyes of many folks. Was he a terrorist operative intending to participate in another hijacking? Or, was he intending, as an aircraft mechanic, to use access to an aircraft to emplace a bomb?

The Rizk case increased the workload for law enforcement. Now, in addition to searching for drugs as they have for decades, priorities shifted requiring them to search for weapons, explosives and now... people.

In March of 2002, authorities identified another container with human cargo. Three individuals from Romania hid within a container leaving a Spanish port. Once the ship departed, it traveled to Halifax, through New Jersey and ended at the Port of Savannah, GA. Even though I was working in another geographic area, I had built a good law enforcement network and received a call from a contact at the Georgia Bureau of Investigations on this one.

The thing that caught my attention was the departing port in Spain. I have been saying for years that we need to look closer at that region. Morocco is a short distance away and Spain is an easy entry point for terrorists seeking to stow away on vessels bound for the west. I'm not sharing any secrets. A little open source research shows that Morocco has an intimate history with Al-Qaeda. I began looking at the maritime routes from Spain to the U.S. and expressed concerns regarding these vessels departing the Middle East/North Africa (MENA) region eventually heading to U.S. waters.

Even though I was the Chief of Intelligence at a small Marine Safety Office in Mobile, AL for the Coast Guard, I had plenty of unwanted oversight by a Navy Civilian working in New Orleans at the time. Whenever I mentioned my concerns, I was told to concentrate "only on my area." I believed then, as I do now that idea is an unintelligent path to travel. Expecting success while operating with blinders only allows the terrorist a significant advantage.

According to the International Maritime Organization (IMO), there were 889 stowaways in 2007 alone. Of those, 25 cases had human cargo within containers. To be fair, the reports show that there were 180 cases onboard Ro-Ro cargo ships. A Ro-Ro is a roll-on/roll-off ship that carries vehicles. These vessels typically have easy access to stowaways because they could hide within vehicles. Another interesting point within the IMO stowaway report are the nationalities of those illegally hiding onboard ships. In 2007, there were 347 stowaways from Afghanistan, 146 from Iraq and 48 from the MENA region. At the time of this writing, we are still amidst armed conflicts in both Afghanistan and Iraq. Stowaways from those countries may be seeking to leave the violence, or some may have a different intent.

Maritime shipping continues to expand and as I said earlier, it is the best economic means to move cargo. Today's freight ships are built larger to carry more containers. Yet, we are short on law enforcement resources to cover the number of threats. If we are not careful, the economic boom for shipping can lead to a bust for law enforcement striving to do their jobs. There are sensor technologies openly available that we can use to detect hidden human cargo. We need to incorporate those into our detection systems.

A Review

We started this chapter looking at the vast amount of losses our economy faces through cargo theft. The multitude of cargo containers entering this country makes for easy targeting by the criminal element. We saw that after the 9/11 terror attack, our law enforcement capabilities were diverted to homeland security issues. In effect, in some areas, we are now less capable to effectively respond and counter the threat of lost cargo and containers within our borders because of inadequate resources. Many criminal groups will opt to steal the entire container rather than pilfer the contents. These stolen cargo boxes could be traveling anywhere along our highways. When we to lose control of the whereabouts of a container, we give the control to others. They may opt to fill it with an explosive device and detonate it in populated areas.

We examined five potential attack scenarios against containerships via small boats, a hijacking, and conventional explosives against the ship, the cargo, and then finally a WMD event. We have seen the propensity to use cargo containers as a vehicle for transferring human cargo. A weapon always needs a trigger. A member of a terrorist group migrating into the country through the maritime nexus might be the source directing the weapon.

Anthony M. Davis

While serving in maritime law enforcement, I came to recognize that international alien migration and narcotics smuggling are similar businesses. When you have a migrant case, you rarely have drugs, unless it is for personal use, and vice versa. When I say they are similar, it is because both criminal enterprises are well organized, they have a unique internal intelligence capability; they make a great deal of money and often operate using the same methods and routes. They typically do not operate in the same areas at the same time. Given that, you have to wonder about communication and agreements between trans-national criminal groups not to tread during the others' route. At the very beginning of this book, I discussed the transparency between criminals and terrorists. Criminals have been using containers for their gain for decades; why wouldn't a terrorist?

Section 3

Other Issues of Concern

Chapter Fifteen

Alien Invaders

They invade our nation every day, early in the morning, late at night and often right before our eyes. These alien invaders enter unseen as they creep into our waters. They are the perfect terrorist causing environmental damage, economic havoc, agricultural destruction, illness, injury and death. Each day these biotic and non-indigenous alien species are released along our coasts in the form of ballast water. This is the cost of doing business.

This chapter is not intended as a science primer and you as a reader might wonder about the relevance to terrorism. Bear with me. The narrative ahead should show that the terrorism possibilities are clear.

While international shipping on one hand brings economic prosperity, it also acts as a dangerous conduit with costly repercussions. As we proceed, we will examine the enormity and consequences of ballast water on a global and national scale. We will look at the purpose of ballast water onboard commercial ships, the entrance routes of aquatic invaders and some potential ways ahead.

The International Maritime Organization estimates that 10 billion tons of ballast water is carried around the world each year by commercial vessels. Of that amount, 79 million tons are dumped into U.S. waters. According to the State Environmental Research Center, approximately 40,000 gallons of contaminated water is released along our coastlines each minute of every day.

Ballast water is an important element for ships to remain stable in the changing ocean environment. To ensure the stability, ships fill ballast tanks with large quantities of seawater. As cargo or fuel loads vary, vessels draw in and release this water back to the sea. While doing so, the potential exists to transfer microbial substances from one geographic region of the world to another.

This ballast when released into our waters may have come from virtually any other geographic region of the world. In fact, the origin may (or may not) have the same health or environmental standards as the United States. These biotic invaders in effect become a threat to the health of our citizens, living marine resources and our nation's economic state.

A brochure published by the U.S. Coast Guard, describes the magnitude of the ballast water threat:

"Every day, large quantities of ballast water from all over the world are discharged into United States waters. Along with this water are plants, animals, bacteria, and pathogens. These organisms range in size from microscopic to large plants and free-swimming fish. These organisms have the potential to become aquatic nuisance species (ANS). ANS may displace native species, degrade native habitats, spread disease, and disrupt human social and economic

activities that depend on water resources. Any ship carrying ballast water is a potential invasion source. "

The Invaders

Biologists believe the Zebra Mussel (Dreissena polymorpha) entered the U.S. in the early 1980's as ballast water hitchhikers in a commercial ship arriving from Europe to the Great Lakes. This bivalve clam has a long history stretching back as far as the 1700's. Originally from Western Asia, it began to invade European waters. Their numbers quickly proliferated, overtaking the riverbeds, lakes and canals. Today they are found throughout all European inland water systems.

In the U.S., they have no natural predators and reproduce at an alarming rate. They spawn twice a year with each female producing up to 100,000 eggs per year. Some areas within the Great Lakes report concentrations of as many as 30,000 of these mollusks per square meter. They quickly overtake underwater structures, pipelines, and power and communication lines. They clog intake pipes delivering water for fire hydrants and cooling for nuclear power plants.

In 1989, the Zebra Mussel attacked the 24,000 residents of Monroe, Michigan. For two days, the city went without water. Because of the Zebra Mussel's rapid growth rate, they clogged the city's water intake pipes. Schools and commercial businesses closed until the pipes could be cleaned of these invaders. The cost of the 1989 invasion was over $300,000.

The rapid propagation of the Zebra Mussel makes control costly and unmanageable. These bivalves spread across the floors of water systems interrupting the natural eco-system, ultimately killing or disrupting native aquatic life. Commercial fishing traps and nets became overrun and were damaged or irretrievable. As a maritime navigation hazard, they cling to buoys and navigational markers, often causing them to sink. Their quickly spreading population presents the possibility of increased maritime accidents, deaths and injuries.

Recreation and tourism also fall victim to the Zebra Mussel. The extremely sharp edges have injured scuba divers and swimmers. In some cases, they completely obscure sunken vessels, effectively shutting down recreational diving businesses. These mollusks colonize on rocks, piers and seawalls near shorelines. As they die and decompose, the odor leaves once flourishing recreational and swimming areas abandoned.

Recreational and charter boat operators face damaged engines and clogged cooling intake lines caused by the Zebra Mussel. They damage fiberglass bottoms and wooden hulls and they increase vessel drag, increasing fuel costs.

A study of associated control costs of the Zebra Mussel for 1989-2000 by the Global Ballast Water Management Programme placed an impact of $750 million to $1 billion U.S. dollars annually. A recent updated estimate by the New York Sea Grant confirms the impact of the Zebra Mussel costs at approximately $1 billion for the period of 1989 to 2005.

Cholera

In 1991, Cholera (Vibrio Cholerae) came to Mobile, Alabama. Two commercial freighters, one from Brazil, another from Colombia entered the Port of Mobile from Latin America bringing with them not only cargo but also the illness-producing strain of cholera. Tests of these vessels confirmed the deadly bacterium resided within the ballast and water holding tanks and the ships' onboard fire-fighting system. During the same year, cholera was found in fin-fish and oyster population within Mobile Bay. Commercial fishing areas were in turn closed by the State of Alabama.

During the same year, a cholera epidemic began in Peru originating from the ballast water of a South Asian commercial ship. Between 1991 and 1995, this pandemic spread throughout Central and South America and into parts of Mexico. Over 1 million people were infected, killing 10,453. I remember very well the precautions taken in the early 1990's while working in Peru. Drinking water was diluted with chlorinated bleach and all vegetables were soaked in a bleach-water mix as a prevention against ingesting the bacteria.

According to Ann Swanson, Executive Director of the Chesapeake Bay Commission, *"The Chesapeake Bay is the largest single recipient of Ballast water on the East Coast."* This key body of water is the entranceway to commercial ships from as many as 48 different foreign ports.

During a pathogen study conducted by the Smithsonian Environmental Research Center (SERC), the ballast water of 15 commercial ships were tested within the Chesapeake Bay. All 15 ships had concentrations of the vibrio cholerae bacteria. According to the SERC study, the Chesapeake Bay receives:

"...some ten billion litres of foreign ballast water

> *each year. Each litre typically contains about a billion bacteria and seven billion virus-like particles."*

Fire Ants

In 1918, the Black Imported Fire Ant (Solenopsis richteri), entered the United States through ballast water in the port of Mobile, Alabama from an Argentinean cargo ship. A few years later, the Red Imported Fire Ant (Solenopsis invicta), being the most dangerous followed the same path of the previous invader through ballast water into the port of Mobile Bay.

Since their arrival, this insect has spread throughout the southern states infesting more than 320 million acres, taking residence in 14 states and Puerto Rico. Estimated damage and control costs for the U.S. are in the billions of dollars annually. According to the Texas Imported Fire Ant Research and Management Project, the impact of the Red Imported Fire Ant is $1.2 billion dollars annually in Texas alone. Hundreds of millions of dollars are spent annually just attempting to control the population.

So far, we have looked at a quick overview of only three examples of the consequences from uncontrolled ballast water entering our waters. Without difficulty, this chapter could easily continue and describe the control and damage costs of potentially thousands of different biotic and non-indigenous alien species.

As final examples, the following are just a few invaders released along our coasts each day through ballast water:

- Formosan termite: ($1 Billion annual cost).

- Toxic algae: ($75 Million annual cost),
- Pfiesteria: (This bacterium causes liver damage, cardiovascular, Intestinal and neurological illnesses and sometimes death.)

Regulation

Because of the potential threats of ballast water, a series of legislative actions occurred beginning with the Nonindigenous Aquatic Nuisance and Prevention Control Act (NANPCA) in 1990. Six years later, the National Invasive Species Act of 1996 was enacted.

In February 1999, President Clinton signed Executive Order 13112 – Invasive Species. This order established the Invasive Species Council with members from the following governmental representatives:

- Secretary of State
- Secretary of the Treasury
- Secretary of Defense
- Secretary of the Interior
- Secretary of Agriculture
- Secretary of Commerce
- Secretary of Transportation
- Administrator of the Environmental Protection Agency

The formation of this council speaks volumes for the seriousness of ballast water when one reviews the membership and the agencies they represent. The council seeks answers to protecting the economy, agriculture and the environment. Ironically, given the potential health concerns, neither the U.S. Department of Health and Human Services nor their subsidiary, Centers for Disease Control was included on the committee. This council was formed *after* the Cholera epidemic years earlier.

Current regulation found in Title 33 of the Code of Federal Regulations, Part 151 requires that vessels traveling beyond the Exclusive Economic Zone (200 Miles from shore) conduct a ballast water exchange. This exchange is generally considered cycling water through the ballast tanks at least three times for at least a 95 percent volumetric exchange.

However, what about vessels that remain within the 200 mile limit? Oil Tankers operating on a coastwise route are currently exempt from the regulation. It becomes far too costly for cruise ships and other commercial cargo carriers traveling along the coast to travel out to sea 200 miles, exchange ballast water and return.

While many of these vessels operate near the coastline, their last port of call may have been Central or South America. Remember the cholera incident? Current ecosystems near ports in California, Oregon and Washington are permanently affected by non-indigenous species originating from these same regions.

During periods of inclement weather, the Ship's Master will often claim, "Force Majeure", claiming that a safety of life at sea issue precludes a trip out to sea to conduct the ballast water exchange. Yet, when the ship enters port and exchanges cargo, the stability of the vessel changes and ballast water is often released into the local waters. There are situations where the weather will alter a ship's voyage, but economics are always an important consideration of the shipper. If they can avoid expending the fuel to venture out to sea for a ballast exchange, they often times will.

If a commercial shipping company violates regulation, they are subject to a civil penalty. The regulation continues to describe how the vessel is liable in rem, meaning the ship can be seized. Even though it is written in regulation, it doesn't happen. No one wants to impede maritime commerce.

In reality, the civil penalty process is broken. As a prior marine investigator, this author saw too many instances of blatant violations of maritime laws and the perpetrators continued without penalty. A thorough case preparation is intense and time consuming, often taking months to bring to adjudication. After revamping case preparation standards, our investigations department began receiving substantial judgments against violators. Even so, we weren't prepared for the "Who knows who" system within the maritime industry. While punitive actions are often ordered, large penalties are often not paid and vessels rarely seized unless there is a political gain behind the move.

Often times, the Coast Guard Captain of the Port will issue a Letter of Concern – nothing more than a slight scolding with no teeth. If too much pressure is placed on a shipper bringing cargo to one port, they will alter future voyages and bring cargo to other, more lenient ports in the region. This affects the local economy and doesn't bode well for those attempting to enforce the law.

Since existing enforcement is lacking, other options are needed, including supplementary ballast water exchange programs, ballast water treatment systems or detection methodologies. Pier side ballast water treatment systems could exchange water as needed according to stability requirements of the vessel due to fuel or cargo changes. The offloaded water would then be sterilized with UV light, sent through micro-particle screens and re-introduced into the port.

Several companies are experimenting with onboard Ballast Water Treatment Systems. One manufacturer, OptiMarin A/S of Norway successfully tested an onboard system on the Princess Cruise line vessel, *Regal Princess*. Using their patented MicroKill ultraviolet light treatment system and the MicroKill cyclonic separator, ballast water was treated with no interruption to any of the ship's operations. The compact size of onboard treatment system uses existing ballast water piping, minimizing costs.

Numerous universities and scientists are beginning to experiment with new bio-detection tools. Many of these are the result of the focus on the threat of terrorism. Their aim is to counter an aerosolized biological attack. Many of these sensors are placed throughout the nation for this reason. If a biological attack were to occur, strategies are in place for the many of the right agencies to respond. Yet, there is no detection plan, response measures or effective enforcement for waterborne, non-indigenous aquatic species. Given our unfortunate level of preparation, treatment systems currently appear to be the most effective solution to this problem.

Lawmakers unwilling to pursue effective regulation hinder the solution. As noted earlier, if pressure is placed upon a shipper, they will move to another port. Ballast Water Treatment Systems should be required for any vessel entering the U.S. after traveling a foreign route. The western states of California, Oregon and Washington have been proactive in recent years by adopting a series of regulations for ballast water exchange and treatment.

Even so, these regulations are not consistent with each other, making compliance difficult for the shipper.

Our nation needs a consistent federal regulation that is actively enforced, requiring Ballast Water Treatment Systems of vessels entering our waters. Yet, this step will place an expectation on our lawmakers to look away from powerful special interest groups supporting the commercial shipping industry. Consistent federal regulations ease compliance and help dictate enforcement. This initiative will not repair years of damage, but it may prevent the continuing threat of non-indigenous aquatic species.

Early in this chapter, I said that you as the reader might wonder about the relevance between alien species and terrorism. We have seen how alien species originating via ballast water have an impact on the environment, national economic base, and agriculture and can cause illness, injury and death. I am not suggesting adversaries brought these to our shores. Nor is there a suggestion that we should limit our international trade through the maritime conduit. Maritime trade is vital to our nation and the overall global economic health. The point: This unregulated gateway provides the potential for the introduction of biological destruction.

When combating an adversary you identify vulnerabilities and then, exploit them. If there are no weaknesses, you create them. In this chapter, we have seen the resulting damage to vital infrastructure (water, nuclear power, and communication lines), the environment and our nation's agricultural food base, and the strength of the overall national economy. It is not impractical to suggest that our adversaries would consider this portal to meet their agenda. If an adversary can hurt our economy, they hurt our national capability to defend ourselves.

In the few examples given within this chapter, we have identified over $2 billion in damage and control costs annually. This is $2 billion that we are not spending on homeland defense. The 2007 Government-Wide Non-Defense Homeland Security budget calls for $41.6 billion. Using a comparative example from the actual accounting budget, the $2 billion lost on damage and control costs by ballast water introduced species would have paid for the entire budgets of the Secret Service and all Science and Technology projects within the Department of Homeland Security during 2007.

Without consistent regulation, fast-acting detection and reporting mechanisms every foreign vessel entering U.S. waters poses potential dangers to the nation's health, welfare, food supplies and economic commerce of the United States.

As commercial shipping trade increases, so does the growing threat of dangerous biotic invaders entering our own shores. The flow of foreign water and substances may not be in the spotlight of terrorist threats. Yet, this threat introduced via a maritime delivery system continues to pose serious consequences.

Chapter Sixteen

Roads, Rail and Infrastructure

In preceding chapters, we looked at a variety of issues dealing with the maritime industry and the potential threats we face from criminal or terrorist elements. The Maritime Transportation System (MTS) is a crucial Intermodal component, which maintains the economic wealth of our nation. So far, we have addressed some of the many challenges our first responders face and viewed specific threats from a maritime perspective. We now need to look at the intermodal links that affect the safe transport of cargo from the ship to the consumer.

The Maritime Transportation System is more than just ships and boats. As I described earlier, our nation has 95,000 miles of coastline and 361 maritime ports of call. Each of these ports in some way or another utilizes portions of the MTS. For many, cargo departs the vessel and is moved to rail systems or hauled by truck. Vessels carry fuels, oils, chemicals or other liquid cargoes. The product pumps directly to pipeline systems for routing to storage tanks around the country. Some cargoes transfer from larger vessels to smaller inland barges capable of navigating waterways inaccessible to ships.

These various transfer protocols make use of our highways, locks, dams, rivers, bridges, tunnels and pipelines. Criminals and terrorists recognize many of the challenges faced by law enforcement to ensure critical infrastructure protection. Our adversaries read the papers, watch the news and scan the internet looking for vulnerabilities. With handheld GPS receivers, online mapping and imagery programs terrorist planners can specify geo-coordinates of infrastructure and identify avenues of approach (and escape) for an attack against these vital elements of the MTS. As we will see in a later view of pipelines, these readily available technologies were incorporated into attack planning.

The Roads and Rails

According to the Federal Motor Carrier Safety Administration (FMCSA), there are over 4.9 million commercial trucks operating on highways within the U.S. In the earlier chapter dealing with cargo theft, we saw that there are times when thieves would rather steal the entire truck and container than risk detection and arrest.

Aside from the potential cargo loss, history shows trucks are an effective and deadly explosive delivery mechanism. They can carry a large amount of explosives as they maneuver through populated areas. On February 22, 1990, Dean Harvey Hicks attempted to detonate a truck bomb loaded with 2,000 pounds of ammonium nitrate fuel oil, parked outside the Internal Revenue Service in Los Angeles. According to the transcript of the official sentencing memorandum, the bomb would have destroyed two city blocks, left a 40-foot wide crater in the street and injured or killed multiple victims. Mr. Hicks received a 20-year prison sentence and $307,452 in fines and restitution.

In October 1983, a truck bomb killed 241 U.S. Marines in Beirut during an attack aimed at the barracks. Eleven months later another attack in the same city killed 24 when a truck exploded near the Embassy annex. The 1993 truck bombing of the World Trade Center killed six. Two years later 168 men, women and children died from the truck bombing of the Alfred P. Murrah Building in Oklahoma City. Terrorists targeted U.S. Air Force personnel 14-months later with a truck bomb at Khobar Towers in Saudi Arabia killing 19. Finally, the coordinated truck bomb attacks against the U.S. Embassies in Nairobi and Tanzania killed 224.

These seven truck bombs killed 672. Yet, they were much smaller than those carrying cargo containers on our streets and highways today. A large truck loaded with explosives can have up to a 60,000-pound explosive capacity and a blast radius of 7,000 feet. With even the best security standards, it is unreasonable to expect a standoff distance of nearly one and half miles from critical infrastructure and key buildings.

With trucks constantly in motion around our nation, how do we identify the potential for attack amidst the nearly 5 million trucks operating along our roadways? Throughout this book, I have made a point to refer to the challenges faced by our law enforcement and intelligence personnel. Unless specific tip-offs are provided beforehand, we may never know of a potential strike until after the fact. As we have seen in the cargo chapter, the vast number of containers entering the country and the expectation of swift freight movement eliminates the full assurance of security. Rather than repeat the discussion from earlier chapters, we will look at the cargo container from a perspective *outside* the port facility gates.

Immediately after the 9/11 attacks, all commercial air flights ceased. From a response perspective, this made sense. The attacks were effectuated via aircraft and we didn't know the full extent of the situation. Were there other flights intended for additional assaults? Who was behind the attacks? If there are more, what are the targets? While the 9/11 Commission report shows there was ongoing concern about Usama bin Laden, in September 2001, all we knew for sure was the targeting mechanism was a commercial aircraft. We were facing cooperation and contingency issues that were failing. The military response was based on cold war methodologies that sent aircraft out to sea rather than to the targeted cities. Leadership needed to regroup and respond to existing attacks rather than risk additional hits.

If terrorists conduct coordinated strikes against the Maritime Transportation System, we will likely replay the same "All-Stop" methodology from September 2001. The economic impact from ceasing cargo movement will exceed the cost of freezing commercial aircraft operations.

The following is a fictional scenario. Imagine that you are a Law Enforcement intelligence analyst. As events unfold, the FBI provides you with additional information fed from the intelligence community. Ten cargo containers exit separate maritime ports around the country. Most were inspected and released for transfer; each is traveling greater than 700 miles to the final delivery point. Three of the containers transfer to rail systems; the rest are shipped by truck. Within the next 24 hours, each truck and train carrying the containers explodes near populated areas. Five of the truck blasts are in the midst of populated highways and two are at fuel stations. The rail attacks occurred on a combination rail/auto bridge, inside a tunnel and at a passenger train depot.

Forensic evidence shows that each of the containers transferred to rail systems originated from the maritime ports of Savannah, Mobile and Oakland. Those containers shipped by truck departed from the ports of Baltimore, Boston, Charleston, Galveston, Houston, New Orleans and Tacoma. Only two of the containers departed the same foreign port of Rotterdam.

The FBI being the authority for domestic terrorism declares that we are facing a coordinated attack and the only links are the maritime ports of entry. The Coast Guard takes action and routes all inbound cargo ships to offshore anchorages until given the clearance to enter. Cargo operations at all ports stop and none leave container yards until fully inspected. Rail service halts nationally. However, truck drivers do not have a coordinated communication or warning system other than word of mouth via cellphone calls or AM/FM or CB radio. Law enforcement and National Guard personnel scramble to set up roadblocks and inspection stations. In a 24-hour period, all maritime commerce ceased.

As an analyst, you face some of the following questions:

- Who is responsible for these attacks?

- Given the 9/11 attacks by Al-Qaeda, is this a coordinated attack by them, another terrorist entity loyal to Al-Qaeda or could it be a domestic group?

- Did the terrorists use ships to deliver the bombs? If so, why were they not detected by inspection? Are insiders at maritime ports involved? If so, how did so many gain access and who are they?

- If the bombs were loaded into containers outside the maritime ports, how and where did this occur?

- What do all the target sites have in common? (Originating country, cargo types, delivery locations, etc)

- Is there anything pertinent to this particular date?

- Are the shipping containers associated with a particular shipping company or a variety of shippers?

- Is the explosive residue from the blasts or the triggering devices related? If so, how?

- What are other potential targets given the events within the last 24-hours?

- What recommendations will you make as an analyst regarding response and contingency operations?

These are just a few of the hundreds of questions that will need answers in a very short time.

So what happened? None of the containers were loaded with explosives while on the ship or before they left the port facility. In fact, none of the containers exploded. Terrorists attached explosive devices using small magnet parasitic boxes to the bottoms of trailers.

Insiders at the rail yards attached devices in the same manner. The intent of the entire operation was designed to simulate attacks originating from ships. This concept was intended to focus law enforcement attention in another direction, thereby allowing a better chance to escape into hiding.

The terrorists waited outside port facilities for trucks with out of state license plates carrying a cargo container clearly marked with a logo from maritime shipping companies. Out of state trucks increased the chances that the cargo was traveling a longer distance and the trucker would eventually stop at a truck stop. The terrorists followed behind the containers to truck stops and attached the devices. Once on the road the terrorists again trailed behind, looking for a target of opportunity. The rail cars had personnel standing by at specific targets. Each device was remotely detonated. None of the attacks came from Al-Qaeda, but each were the work of domestic environmental groups opposing the use of fossil fuels.

The point from this exercise is to illustrate how closely interrelated elements of the intermodal transportation system are. When an event occurs in one sphere, it becomes easy to affect other portions of the system. In the narrative above, we have seen that the Coast Guard was able to assume positive control of shipping. The rail systems each have dedicated communication systems capable of sending a warning. Yet, with nearly five million trucks operating throughout our highway systems, we rely on phone calls and radios as an emergency contingency plan.

This issue needs addressing. Many commercial trucking firms utilize satellite systems that allow communication between drivers and base stations. Yet, not all trucking companies are equipped with such devices. All major transportation systems should have the ability to receive an emergency broadcast in the event of a terror attack or natural disaster.

Another point of this exercise is to show that while international terrorist groups want to attack us, we also need to keep a focus on domestic groups. If an attack occurs, it is important to view potential motivations related to specific targets. In this scenario, the targets were random, but all related to transportation and fuel use. Our adversary may be within our borders and have access to the Maritime Transportation System.

Anthony M. Davis

The Pipelines

Many cargo ships that carry LNG, petroleum products or chemicals conduct a direct transfer of their product to pipelines rather than ship them by truck or rail systems. For ports that have a pipeline transfer capability, this often allows a safer and more direct route to the final containment areas.

Yet, pipelines are an often-unseen element of the Maritime Transportation System that spreads across our nation. While we may not see them, there are over 2.4 million miles of pipelines below our cities and parallel to our interstate highways. Additionally, there are over 200,000 miles of petroleum pipelines throughout the U.S. Generally, the three main types of pipelines are interstate and intrastate natural gas and hazardous liquids. Yet, in addition to those products moving below ground, there are other volatile substances as well. One pipeline provider, Buckeye Partners, L.P. describes how they own and operate:

> "5,350 miles of underground pipelines serving over 100 delivery locations within eighteen states. The company transports refined petroleum products including gasoline, jet fuel, diesel fuel, heating oil, and kerosene from major supply sources to industry-owned terminals and airports located within major end-use markets. Buckeye also transports other refined products, such as propane and butane."

For the supertankers carrying crude oil from abroad, these tankers are too large for safe navigation along narrow waterways and many inland ports are unable to accommodate their large size. A maritime casualty from one of these vessels would cause catastrophic environmental damage if a spill ensued.

One solution is the Louisiana Offshore Oil Port (LOOP). Stationed in the Gulf of Mexico, the LOOP is the only U.S. offshore port capable of unloading the large deep draft vessels known as the Ultra Large Crude Carriers (ULCC) and Very Large Crude Carriers (VLCC). The LOOP handles approximately 13 percent of the nation's imported crude oil and transfers 1.2 million barrels of crude each day through 48-inch pipeline connections. The LOOP has connections to over 50 percent of the nation's refinery capacity.

Pipelines operate under the oversight of the Office of Pipeline Safety (OPS). Statistics show that during the period of 1987 to 2006, there were 5,797 significant pipeline incidents within the U.S. Property damages exceeded $3.2 billion, killing 417 and 1,832 injured. Even so, while pipeline operators strive to ensure the safe operation and integrity of these vital transport systems, terrorists have recognized their value to the U.S. economy, as we will see ahead.

In January 2007, law enforcement arrested Russell Defreitas, a 63-year old former JFK Airport employee, for his part in planning to destroy the airport, tower, adjoining fuel tanks and pipelines along the jet fuel pipeline. Years ago, while working at the airport, he saw what he believed to be U.S. missiles loaded onto aircraft bound for Israel. Through a confidential source, law enforcement maintained surveillance of Defreitas and activities as he traveled between New York, Guyana and Trinidad seeking support of the Trinidadian Muslim group Jamaat Al Muslimeen (JAM) for the attacks. Both Defreitas and the source conducted video surveillance of the facilities and reviewed targets using the Google Earth software-mapping program.

The main emphasis of the attacks was the destruction of the 40-mile Buckeye pipeline that transports jet fuel from the Linden, NJ containment facility to the JFK Airport. According to Port Authority experts cited with the Federal criminal complaint, over 1,000 passenger and cargo aircraft transit through the airport on a typical day. The transcript continues to state that in 2007, 45 million passengers and $120 billion of cargo transited through the airport. According to Defreitas, "Only a few people would escape and that due to the underground piping, part of Queens would explode." If such an attack occurred, there could be an enormous cost of lives and a direct blow to both the U.S. and the international economy from the delay of air cargo bound for foreign countries.

While news reporting of this planned attack described it as being potentially devastating, the reality is that these people failed to consider that the infrastructure has built-in safety protocols that would prevent the disaster envisioned within Defreitas' mind. There is no doubt that if he had gained access to the airport and emplaced bombs near the tower, fuel tanks and pipelines, some damage would result.

There would likely be localized fires to the facilities and fuel areas. Nevertheless, given the many safety cutoffs along the line, the damage would be isolated to the areas of the blasts. Flights from the airport would be delayed or cease temporarily until law enforcement and safety inspectors could ensure no follow-on attacks. Given that, the economy would take a hit and the event classified as a terror attack against transportation and infrastructure.

A Review

In the beginning of this chapter, we began by looking at the intermodal mechanisms that are part of the Maritime Transportation System. We have seen that there are 4.9 million commercial trucks operating on highways within the U.S.

It is important to note that these are just those commercial trucks registered in the U.S. We additionally face cross-border issues as we allow trucks to enter our southern borders from Mexico. How safe are these vehicles? Do we know the background of the drivers? Are they associated with criminal or terrorist elements? Will these trucks be used to smuggle drugs or other contraband into the country? Will they be used to smuggle laundered money out of the country? In the chapter, *Criminals and Terrorists*, I discussed how transnational criminal groups exploit the borderless society formed by trade agreements. We face difficult challenges keeping people from walking across our borders; how can we be sure the trucks driving across are safe?

We saw the deadly effect of seven bombs against U.S. citizens and see that an explosive-laden commercial truck leaves devastating results. The fictional scenario showed us that a coordinated attack using cargo containers transported by truck and rail could halt the Maritime Transportation System. I was hesitant to portray this scenario, as I don't want to be accused of giving terrorists ideas. Then, as described in earlier chapters, terrorists don't need my help. Hollywood and many fiction writers provide viewers with plenty of potential scenarios. This book however, exposes a serious communication issue regarding commercial trucks. If there is no established emergency broadcast methodology to coordinate the nearly 5 million trucks on our highways, then that is a problem that needs addressing.

In the fictional scenario, we saw that the threat came from within our borders by domestic terrorists and not from an Al-Qaeda related organization. We saw an example of an internal threat by Dean Harvey Hicks when he attempted a deadly terrorist attack in Los Angeles using a truck bomb. It is vital that we always consider our threats from within our borders. When Russell Defreitas sought to attack our pipelines, intending to kill and destroy our infrastructure, that attack would have caused serious damages to commerce if successful. Fortunately, his concocted plan would likely not meet his expectations.

As an after-the-fact look, another issue arises that continually challenges our law enforcement capability to prevent such an incident. Watchdog groups and propagandists are protesting the government's use of the source that reported the information. In this case, the source was convicted for drug trafficking and crimes under the Racketeer Influenced and Corrupt Organizations (RICO) Act. The facts are clear. The source does have a criminal history. Yet, he provided the government with recordings, emails, documents and a variety of corroborated information. Surveillance tapes indicated that Defreitas was the planner and actively engaged in trying to kill Americans, destroy infrastructure and harm our economy.

We are fighting a war against those wanting to kill the innocent. At the beginning of this book, I described the transparency between criminals and terrorists. It is often the criminal that will have the knowledge and access to the terrorist elements seeking to do us harm. Many of these watchdog groups need to get away from their "group hug" mentalities and get onboard with the reality that terrorists do not care much for them nor their families. If the criminal element can provide corroborated information to prevent an attack, we should use them. This incident illustrates there are plenty out there seeking to attack us and elements of the Maritime Transportation System provide plenty of opportunities.

A Final Review

We began this book by looking at the maritime nexus and how collectively, the intermodal mechanisms used for the transfer of cargo from the shipper to the consumer becomes known as the Maritime Transportation System. It is more than just ships, boats and coasts. We see the maritime industry relies upon the ability of other transportation sectors to complete the task of delivery. While some cargo moves to trucks, others to rail systems. Liquid cargoes often pump directly to pipelines that sprawl across our nation like an intricate network of arteries.

We have seen that international trade agreements support economic growth and allow transnational criminal organizations new flexibility to operate. While international trade partnerships offer economic opportunity, the borders are in a sense, removed. Criminal and terrorist activity sometimes becomes transparent and difficult to define the line separating the two. Criminal organizations recognized centuries ago that the maritime nexus is an effective tool at their disposal. In recent years, terrorist groups have caught on to the same concept.

We face a host of challenges in this regard. Key to the successful intervention of a terror attack is an effective law enforcement, intelligence and response posture. We saw that our responders face numerous issues. Many from their own testimony describe issues and frustrations as they strive to keep our nation safe. Reviewing domestic crimes against persons, we saw that given a different perspective and definition of terrorism, separating crime from terror becomes even more complicated. When we are unable to establish a global definition of terrorism at a time when we are fighting the Global War on Terror (GWOT), how can we effectively fight it if we don't know what it is?

Given the historical use of the maritime industry by terrorists, we looked at the vessels and how the age, structural condition and types of cargo transported could give clues to ships of concern. Ironically, we pay attention to the high value, caustic and explosive cargoes. Yet, a vessel that carries low-value cargoes like wood chips might sail in under the radar.

The Coast Guard does a good job of screening inbound ships based on the best and latest information available. I have seen firsthand what they do at the National Maritime Intelligence Center (NMIC). Yet, there is a perception that the job of domestic maritime protection belongs to the Coast Guard alone. Bear in mind, this small multi-faceted service operates worldwide, faces a host of enormous and often dangerous tasks, with a personnel complement smaller than the New York Police Department.

My first Coast Guard Cutter, the *USCGC Spar* was 42-years old when I arrived. It was one of three original vessels to circumnavigate the top of the globe in 1957. Most of their fleet of Medium and Large endurance Cutters are well beyond their useable life. Looking back at the chapter dealing with structural failures and stresses on ships, our Coast Guardsmen and women trust their lives to these ships everyday in harsh sea conditions. New vessels built under the "Deepwater Project" are supposed to alleviate the strain on overused ships and provide new technologies for future operations.

In the end, there will be a smaller fleet and some patrol areas untouched unless the Marine Safety and Security Teams (MSST) grow to new levels. This small, overworked service always seems to get the crumbs of congressional support.

When we looked at the sailors crewing commercial vessels we found that while there are many professionals working within the maritime industry, others found this occupation to be a safe haven. As we have seen, some serial offenders can benefit by using the ease of maritime mobility for new hunting grounds and escape. Until Operation DRYDOCK, if an individual sought to avoid the IRS, their spouse or the law, the maritime industry was an attractive option.

At the close of the multi-agency Task Force, we found thousands of mariners with fraudulent applications, undisclosed criminal records, some with active warrants for their arrest and nine with possible links to terrorism. The Coast Guard has since incorporated new biometric technologies to identify and compare mariners against FBI databases in West Virginia. Unfortunately, the regulations continue to leave loopholes regarding when a criminal background check is required.

We saw that barges become large uncontrolled battering rams when the controlling towboat experiences a steering or propulsion loss. These vessels often carry poisonous or caustic chemicals capable of causing environmental havoc if the barge suffers a breached hull. The two maritime casualties discussed, the CSX Bridge near Mobile, Alabama and the Interstate 40 Bridge new Webbers Falls, Oklahoma show that sometimes location does not matter. Whether the bridge is in a remote area or readily visible makes little difference when barges and towboats go out of control and strike transportation structures used by commuters, passengers and the delivery of cargo.

As we moved to the freight and tank ships, we saw these to be larger, more deadly battering rams. Once again, looking at two bridges we see the potential for catastrophe when a vessel loses the capability of safe navigation through narrow channels. Because of the sheer size and quantity of product carried in a large tanker, a spill quickly becomes an environmental disaster. Both the *Exxon Valdez* and the *Westchester* shows that a spill influences the entire U.S. economy when vital maritime routes close due to response operations.

Additionally, an environmental disaster hurts the local regional economy and diverts maritime security resources, leaving gaps in our national maritime security posture. We have seen that smuggling is another issue with larger vessels for transnational criminal groups. Law enforcement can only do a quick check for drugs and human smuggling unless intelligence provides a solid tip. Even then, if no contraband or migrants are found it becomes an issue when a vessel is detained. When a ship stops operating, the shipping company loses money and they complain to those in power. The law enforcement personnel seeking to do a good job will eventually hear about it.

The chapter dealing with small boat attacks shows us these vessels are often very effective when it comes to conducting a maritime terror attack. This proved true with both the *MV Limburg*, the *USS Cole* and a host of Tamil Tiger attacks off the coast of Sri Lanka. The larger the cargo ship, the more difficult to safely navigate through narrow waterways. If a small boat can force a larger ship to slow down in an attempt to avoid a collision, it may lose the valuable forward speed necessary to allow rudder control. If this scenario occurs near a large transportation structure or a rocky coastline, the result may be destruction or grounding, followed by an oil spill. In either event, the waterway closes, preventing maritime commerce and the event gains news coverage. Such a consequence might pay out larger dividends to a terrorist than a bomb-laden boat.

Our look at piracy shows that some parts of the maritime world are out of control. Fortunately, many of those events are away from U.S. shores. Yet, we should not be so ignorant to think that the problem belongs to someone else in somebody else's waters. U.S. and Western Allies continually become targets of piracy, hijackings and ransom demands increase. While some attacks go unreported to prevent rising insurance premiums, someone always pays the cost. With each attack, the confidence of safe maritime transit wanes and shippers seek safer routes to operate. Those regions losing a maritime commerce capability then become impoverished and beholden to the international community for aid and monetary support. This cycle once started, becomes difficult to reverse. International crime networks controlling and supporting piracy operations eventually become stronger than enforcement agencies seeking to control the pirates. This is a mentality often mirrored by terrorist organizations.

Some describe Liquefied Natural Gas (LNG) vessels with unsubstantiated fears. Certainly, there are dangers associated with these vessels, but without understanding the facts and a look at survivable response measures, failure waits around the corner.

We have seen that LNG vessels are not the "floating bombs" that some portray. When the gas is super-cooled to -260 degrees Fahrenheit, the gas does not burn, nor does it explode. This chapter dug a little deep into the technical details, but frankly, it was necessary for accuracy and to express the dangers that do exist when responding to an LNG incident.

If those loyal to Usama bin Laden heed his 1991 fatwa to kill Americans, we should then be mindful that large passenger vessels become prime targets. The chapter discussing High Occupancy Vessels gives us some historical examples where terrorists incorporated these ships into their attacks. It is unreasonable to expect passenger vessel operators to limit their passenger counts in the event a terrorist might decide to attack. Such a result becomes a success for the terrorist without any action on their part. The only reasonable option at this point is a well-trained security force, biometric identification and commercial off-the-shelf scanning systems. None comes without a hefty price.

Fishing vessels are one of those areas where there are holes in the system. In the chapter dealing with the sailors that crew cargo ships, we looked at the basic proficiencies required to earn a Merchant Mariners' Document (MMD). We saw that regulation established enforcement mechanisms and requires oversight to ensure mariners are drug-free. This is not the case with the many fishing vessels. In fact, we have seen no requirements for criminal background checks or drug tests of operators.

Many reputable fishing vessel operators work

hard each day to earn a living. Nevertheless, opportunities avail for illegitimate activities. We have seen historical examples of drug activity. In fact, precursor chemicals used to manufacture methamphetamine are used onboard these boats. Along our coastlines and throughout many inland waterways fishing boat operators earn their wage. Yet, with such little oversight, we do not know who is onboard the vessel, their backgrounds, if they are qualified to safely operate the boat, or whether their activities are legal. How does that scenario fit into an effective maritime security posture?

Containerships, like LNG vessels, are a top subject of maritime security and terrorism discussions. Statistics show there were 19,591 port calls by containerships to U.S. ports. Plainly speaking, that is a lot of cargo. Criminal groups recognize the vast opportunities to steal. Think about it and look around your home or office. Chances are your computer, television, stereo system, the mp3 player you take to the gym, and even the watch on your arm at one time most likely traveled to the distributor in a container. If criminal organizations can gain knowledge of the contents, they may certainly get access once the products leave the port. As we have seen, with an estimated $25 billion in cargo losses each year from theft, our economy takes a daily beating.

For some, this might be a stretch, but using a portion of my earlier definition of terrorism, "*...to wage destruction affecting economic commerce to support an agenda*", is this not in a sense a form of internal terror against our own nation? I can understand disagreement on this point because I am not sure I'm settled with it myself. What it continues to show however is that defining terrorism continues to be a nebulous thing.

Continuing with containers, we looked at five potential terrorism scenarios. With any of the options (small boat attack, hijacking, conventional explosives against the ship, the cargo or a WMD event), our first responders need to be prepared. Law enforcement and the intelligence community should examine each scenario and develop response strategies for their areas. Once these plans are completed, those chains of authority expected to act on them should know what they are.

Over the years, I have spoken with many Emergency Management personnel in various parts of the country. They described working for months drafting response plans in the event of a terror attack. During one conversation, I asked one manager who knew about the plans, whether partnering agencies know where the staging areas are, and understand their responsibilities. As it turned out, the plans were stored in a safe and only a few knew of them. The Incident Commander would receive the plan if an event occurred. Years after the 9/11 attacks, given the communication and response issues faced back then, this "plan" seemed preposterous to me. After some probing questions, the manager admitted that perhaps the plan needed some work.

Today, the incident plans reside in secure locations accessible to the many agencies expected to contribute during an event. The city conducts Incident Management System (ICS) training and response exercises. It is vital that key players know the responsibilities of each agency. To reiterate what I said in an chapter, *"The Incident Command Center is the wrong place to be sharing business cards for the first time."*

There may be times when a terrorist conducts

planning and surveillance under our legal radar. Sometimes the radar is turned off. Intelligence oversight laws prevent the intelligence community from looking within our borders at U.S. persons. Then, some laws restrict domestic surveillance operations by law enforcement. I am not suggesting that is wrong. We live in that legal realm for a reason. Given that we may not be always be able to prevent an incident, we need to be ready to respond if one occurs.

Throughout this book, I have made a consistent point to tie in the economic cost of issues related to the Maritime Transportation System. Foreign vessels enter U.S. waters everyday. Their arrival comes with a consistent risk to the health of our citizens and the eco-system. In an earlier chapter, we saw that non-indigenous species brought into the country by foreign ships once shut down the water system of a Michigan town for two days. Ships entering our ports often bring with them the deadly cholera bacterium.

While ballast water is a necessity of safe vessel operations to maintain stability, many regulatory holes exist. Some U.S. states and the International Maritime Organization have become proactive regarding ballast water exchange and treatment systems. Yet, many of these initiatives lack consistency between regions or are not enforced. Ballast water is not seen as a terrorist threat. Yet, it is a huge global economic drain.

There are no reports that terrorists are seeking to use this as a method to attack us. However, if we fail to incorporate regulatory standards, we continue to pay billions of dollars each year in damage and control costs. These are lost homeland security dollars. If ballast water treatment systems are not mandated leaving the door open to biological havoc, why wouldn't a terrorist eventually recognize that entryway and walk through it?

The final chapter, *Roads, Rails and Infrastructure,* shows how an attack against one area of the Maritime Transportation System in effect influences the rest of the intermodal system. We expect the capability to move cargo from the ports to the consumer quickly. Nonetheless, that expectation requires safe transportation systems and infrastructure.

After the I-35W bridge incident in Minneapolis, we found that much of our national transportation infrastructure is in poorer condition that we would hope. Foreign nationals are driving large trucks through the borders and across our highways and we have little knowledge of their background. Accidents can occur resulting from environmental conditions and mechanical failure of vessels operating near bridge structures. Sometimes we see the destruction of transportation infrastructures because of human factors like the CSX Bridge disaster in Mobile, Alabama. We have seen those living within our borders intending to conduct terror attacks using trucks and pipelines. This internal threat maintains an often-unburdened opportunity to conduct surveillance, purchase supplies and carry out their attacks. Unless law enforcement receives a solid tip-off and can prove probable cause, they lack the legal authority to intervene.

We have looked at 16 chapters that in one form or another address the maritime nexus and those challenges faced by law enforcement. Given that, we are not to live in fear. If we choose that path, the criminal and the terrorists succeed. There are issues noted in this text where we can take action.

We must recognize our own responsibility as citizens to remain cognizant of potential threats around us and participate in the work. Our lawmakers must be held accountable to ensure those striving to keep this nation safe receive the resources to do the job.

I have seen many hard-working men and women trying to make things better. Yet, some above them fear change because change equals unacceptable and personal risk to their careers. As a nation, we need strong leadership. We must be willing to put in the due diligence knowing our hard work may not benefit us, but steer a safe path for those that come after. We benefit today because of those who came before us. We have strong challenges ahead. These are opportunities to extend the legacy of a free, democratic society and the building of a safer nation.

About the Author

Anthony M. Davis is the Founder of the Homeland Security Group and publisher of the Homeland Security Reports, read worldwide by the law enforcement, intelligence, security and emergency management communities.

Mr. Davis is a retired Coast Guard Officer having served as the Intelligence Chief with the USCG Marine Safety Office in Mobile, AL. Upon retiring from the service, he once again served the Coast Guard as a Federal Civilian Maritime Investigator.

He is a member of the International Association of Law Enforcement Intelligence Analysts (IALEIA) and serves on the Training, Education and Career Development Board. Mr. Davis also serves as a member of the International Association of Marine Investigators.

He is a contributing author for the International Analyst Network, recipient of the 2004 IALEIA Professional Service Award and was the 2003 Federal Employee of the Year for Civil Law Enforcement.

Bibliography

American Commercial Lines, Inc. About Us

AntColony.org, Fire Ants

Asian Political News, 3 bodies pulled from Sri Lanka tanker sunk by suicide boat, November 5, 2001.

Benzene.org. Benzene Side Effects

Blair, A., Haas, T., Prosser, R., Morrissette, M., Blackman, K., Grauman, D., et al. (1989, May). Mortality among United States Coast Guard Marine Inspectors. Archives of Environmental Health.

Broughton E. The Bhopal disaster and its aftermath: a review, Environmental Health: A Global Access Science Source [Environ Health], (2005), Vol. 4 (1), pp. 6.

Buckeye Partners, L.P., About Us

CalTrade Report, Terrorist Threat Shuts Down Central California Port June 26, 2006.

Cable News Network, Crews on Mississippi tackle largest oil spill since Exxon Valdez. November 30, 2000.
      ---. Israel strikes back after university bombing. August 1, 2002.

CH-IV International, A Brief History of U.S. LNG Incidents. 2006.

CSX Corporation (2005), Alabama Factsheet.

Council on Foreign Relations. (2003). Emergency Responders: Dangerously Underfunded, Dangerously Unprepared.

Core, Jim. (2003), Hot on the Trail of Fire Ants. Agricultural Research 51, no. 2: 20.

Courtroom Television Network (2003). Double Bombing in Sandy Springs.

Daly, John. Energy Publisher. LTTE: Technologically innovative rebels, June 5, 2007.

Dominion Cove LNG, LP. History of Liquefied Natural Gas.

Economist, Dead Men Tell No Tales, December 18, 1999.

El País, pp. 33-34; Radiografía del ELN, July 5, 1998.

Foss, Michelle M. Ph.D. Center for Energy Economics, LNG Safety and Security. October 2003.

Gale, Ivan. GulfNews.com. US Navy and Somalis 'tracking cargo ship' November 5, 2006.

Gerard, Ian. The Australian. Mini-subs to check ship hulls for drugs. November 8, 2006.

Gillan, Audrey. Guardian News. Guns, grenades and GPS: the brutal reality of Somalia's hi-tech pirates. June 12, 2007.

Global Ballast Water Management Programme, International Maritime Organization.

GlobalSecurity.org. Aden-Abyan Islamic Army.

Gordon, Sandy Dr. (1999). Crime and the Future.

Hitt, Jack. New York Times. Bandits in the Global Shipping Lanes. August 20, 2000.

Human Rights Watch, Appendix One: Chronology Of Attacks.

ICC Commercial Crime Services, International Maritime Bureau, Piracy and Armed Robbery Against Ships. 2006 Annual Report.

---. Global Project Task Force, Fourth Meeting Proceedings, Beijing, China (2002).

---. Piracy Prone Areas.

---. Reported Piracy Incidents Rise Sharply in 2007.

---. Global Project Task Force, Fourth Meeting Proceedings, Beijing, China (2002).

International Criminal Police Review - No 469-471 (1998). The Bombing of the World Trade Center in New York City.

International Maritime Organization, International Convention for the Control and Management of Ship's Ballast Water and Sediments, 13 February 2004.

---. Information Sheet No. 33, Stowaways / Illegal Migrants / Treatment of Persons Rescued at Sea. December 11, 2007.

International Navigational Rules Act of 1977 (Public Law 95-75, 91 Stat. 308, or 33 U.S.C. 1601-1608), and, the Inland Navigation Rules Act of 1980 (Public Law 96-591, 94 Stat. 3415, 33 U.S.C. 2001-2038).

Israel Action Committee, (2002). The use of ambulances and medical material for terror.

Jeyaraj, D.B.S. Indian help sought to escort 'Pearl Cruiser' safely to KKS, May 12, 2006.

KBS World. Mavuno Vessels. November 11, 2006.

Khurana, Gurpreet Singh, China and Eurasia Forum Quarterly, Volume 4, No. 3 (2006) p. 89-103, Central Asia-Caucasus Institute & Silk Road Studies Program, Securing the Maritime Silk Route: Is There a Sin-Indian Confluence?

League of Nations Convention, (1937).

Lorch, Donatella. New York Times, Tucked Above a Rudder: 2 Men and Cocaine, January 19, 1991.

Lohr, David. Richard Speck. Crime Magazine, 20 August 2003.

Louisiana Offshore Oil Port (LOOP), About LOOP.

Marighella, Carlos. (1969). The Minimanual of the Urban Guerilla.

MarketWatch, American Commercial Lines Accelerates Organic Growth Initiatives. (2007).

Marriott, Trevor, Jack the Ripper: The 21st Century Investigation. Blake Publishing.

McLeod, Judi. Canadian Free Press, Drug smugglers hitch rides on Canada Steamship Lines.

National Archives and Records Administration, Federal Register: September 4, 2003 (Volume 68, Number 171), Page 52508-52510.

National Transportation Safety Board, (1982). Aircraft Accident Report No. NTSB-AAR-82-8.

  ---. Derailment of Amtrak Train No. 2 on the CSXT Big Bayou Canot Bridge near Mobile, Alabama, September 22, 1993. Railroad/Marine Accident Report NTSB/RAR-94/01. Washington, DC.

  ---. U.S. Towboat Robert Y. Love Allision With Interstate 40 Highway Bridge Near Webbers Falls, Oklahoma, May 26, 2002. Highway/Marine Accident Report NTSB/HAR-04/05. Washington, DC.

Nilsen, Birgir, OptiMarin AS, personal communication.

Norwegian Maritime Directorate (NMD) report: LEROS STRENGTH, The Classification of a Sunken Ship.

Office of Management and Budget, Department of Homeland Security 2007 Budget.

O'Neill, Charles R., New York Sea Grant, personal communication.

Peace Secretariat of the Liberation Tigers of Tamil Eelam, Official Website. Agreements With The Government of The Democratic Socialist Republic of Sri Lanka.

Pessin, Al. Voice of America. US Navy Gets Tough with Pirates off Somalia. December 21, 2007.

Public Safety Wireless Network, (2002). Answering the Call: Communications Lessons Learned from the Pentagon Attack.

Radio Free Europe, (2003). Russia: Truck-Bomb Attack Kills At Least 35 In Ossetia.

Rhode Island Sea Grant, University of Rhode Island, Graduate School of Oceanography, Zebra Mussel Facysheet.

Ruiz, Gregory M., Rawlings, Tonya K., Dobbs, Fred C., Drake, Lisa A., Mullady, Timothy, Huq, Anwarul, and Rita R. Colwell. 2000. Global spread of microorganisms by ships. *Nature* 408, no. 6808: 49

Safety at Sea, March 1, 2007. Five months for fake ferry Captain.

Sandia National Laboratories, Guidance on Risk Analysis and Safety Implications of a Large Liquefied Natural Gas (LNG) Spill Over Water. pg.51. SAND2004-6258. December 2004.

SeaWeb, Nonindigenous Species and the Marine Environment.

State Environmental Research Center, Foreign Species in Ballast Water: Threat to Our Health, Economy, and Ecosystem.

South Asia Terrorism Portal, Institute for Conflict Management, Sri Lanka Timeline – 2001.

Swanson, Ann P., Executive Director, Chesapeake Bay Commission, Maryland Office. Alien Species in the Chesapeake Bay.

Texas A&M University, Department of Entomology, Texas Imported Fire Ant Research and Management Project.

Text of Usama bin Laden, Fatwah Urging Jihad Against Americans. (1998).

The White House, Office of the Press Secretary. Fact Sheet on Shutting Down the Terrorist Financial Network. December 4, 2001.

Time Magazine, 24 Years to Page One. 29 July 1966.

---. Who Killed King. 26 April 1968.

U.S. Army War College Quarterly, Parameters, Al Qaeda and the Internet: The Danger of "Cyberplanning". Spring 2003.

U.S. Coast Guard, Chemical Hazards Information Response System (CHRIS), 1999.

---. Aquatic Nuisance Species.

---. District Eight Public Affairs. Personal Communication, Visneski, Anastasia, Ltjg.

---. Marine Transportation System Factcard

---. Maritime Information Exchange, Incident Investigation Reports. 2007.

---. U.S. Coast Guard, Search and Rescue Event Log (1996).

U.S. Code of Federal Regulations, Title 28, section 0.85

---. CFR Title 33, Chapter 1, Section 104.105. Maritime Security: Vessels

---. CFR Title 33, Chapter 1, Section 105.245. Declaration of Security (DoS).

---. CFR Title 46 section 12.02-4

---. CFR Title 46 section 16.113

U. S. Code of Law, Title 18, section 2339B.

---. Title 22, section 2656f(d)

---. Title 50, Chapter 35.

---. Title 50, Chapter 36, section 1806(k).

---. Title 50, Chapter 36, section 1825(k)

U.S. Customs Service. U.S. Customs Today, November 2000 Edition.

U.S. Department of Justice, Federal Bureau of Investigation, Congressional Statement. May 18, 2004.

---. Direct Examination of Brian Parr, United States of America v. Ramzi Ahmed Yousef and Eyad Ismoil, S1293CR.180, October 22, 1997, pp. 4734-4735.

---. National Drug Threat Assessment 2001 –
The Domestic Perspective, October 2000.

---. National Drug Threat Assessment,
January 2003.

---. Terrorism in the United States. (1998).

---. Uniform Crime Reports.

U.S. Department of Labor, Occupational Health and Safety
Administration (OSHA), Evacuation Planning Matrix.

U.S. Department of Transportation, Bureau of Transportation
Statistics, Marine Casualty Event Table. 2001.

---. Maritime Data Working Group. Marine
Casualty and Pollution Database, July 2006.

---.Federal Motor Carrier Safety
Administration (FMCSA), Motor Carrier
Safety Fact Sheet.

---. Office of Pipeline Safety, Pipeline and
Hazardous Materials Safety Administration,_
Significant Pipeline Incidents.

United States District Court, Central District of California,
Sentencing Memorandum, CR91-842-LEW, United States of
America v. Dean Harvey Hicks.

United States District Court, Eastern District of New
York. United States of America v. Russell Defrietas, File
#2006R00688.

United States District Court, Southern District of New
York, United States of America v. Usama bin Laden, et al.,
Defendants. February 21, 2001.

U.S. Environmental Protection Agency. Comprehensive
Environmental Response, Compensation, and Liability Act
(CERCLA), 1980.

U.S. Food and Drug Administration, Center for Food Safety &
Applied Nutrition.

---. Holding Tank Waters to be Checked for
Cholera. November, 20, 1991.

U.S. Government Accountability Office. Report No. GAO-NSIAD-96-119, April 1996.

---. Pipeline Safety, GAO-04-801, July 2004.

---. Public Safety Consequences of a Terrorist Attack on a Tanker Carrying Liquefied Natural Gas Need Clarification, GAO-07-316. February 2007.

U.S. House of Representatives, 107th Congress, 1st session, H.R. 3162. USA PATRIOT Act. October 24, 2001.

---. 108th Congress, 1st Session. H.R. 3370. Public Safety Interoperability Implementation Act.

U.S. Immigration and Customs Enforcement, Major Initiatives: ICE Operations in Iraq, March 23, 2004.

United Nations, (1999). International Convention for the Suppression of the Financing of Terrorism.

University of British Columbia, Physical and Chemical Characteristics of Seawater.

US Energy Information Administration, Country Analysis Briefs, World Oil Chokepoints.

Valdezalaska.org. History and Facts.

Watkins, Eric. PennEnergy, Cosco Busan faces over $61 million in Bay cleanup.

White, Gregory J. Dr. Loads on a Ship's Structure. U.S. Naval Academy.

Winchester, Nik, Seafarer's International Research Centre, The Sea, Spotting a Fake is no Simple Matter. November 2005.

Index

Printed in the United States
118752LV00003B/11/P